2nd Edition

FIRESCAPING

Protecting Your Home with a Fire-Resistant Landscape

PRAISE FOR *FIRESCAPING*

"I have to shelter in place with my 1,500 rescued animals in Southern California. In over 30 years, we have weathered many fires, three of them famous. I have an entire fire library, and this is the best book ever for fire protection in the wildland–urban interface. Many of the subjects covered are never even mentioned in the official firefighting training and certification manuals. I am going to give *Firescaping* as a gift to my local fire stations as well as to all my neighbors."
—*Leo Grillo, founder, D.E.L.T.A. Rescue*

"This is the quintessential guide for landscape architects practicing in wildfire-prone regions. There is no better resource for designers of all levels to gain in-depth knowledge of fire science, management practices, and key design skills to create a safer built environment."
—*Blake Rhinehart, PLA, president of the Northern California chapter of the American Society of Landscape Architects and a partner at Urban Arena*

"As a rural mountain resident, first responder, and water conservationist, I thought I had a pretty good foundation on fire protection, but *Firescaping* opened my eyes to how much more there was to learn and do. This is an essential resource for anyone living in or near fire country."
—*Sierra Orr, water conservation and public information supervisor, Big Bear Lake Department of Water and Power*

"The second edition of *Firescaping* has evolved into an exceptionally useful reference for homeowners and landscape professionals alike. The book is clear, concise, and relevant for a wide variety of situations and locations. Through his passion and knowledge, Doug has succeeded in creating an essential reference that will be a valuable resource for years to come."
—*Gregory Plumb, water use efficiency programs specialist, Sonoma Water*

"The threat of wildfires is an inescapable part of reality in California and other parts of the semiarid West. But we can still learn lessons from the mistakes of the past. This up-to-date, clearly written, and user-friendly book gives us the lessons we need to curtail or prevent catastrophes in the future."
—*Michael Woo, dean of the College of Environmental Design, California State Polytechnic University, Pomona, and former Los Angeles city council member and city planning commissioner*

"Our organization works hard to create health and resiliency in California. We provide landscape training to public agencies, landscape professionals, and homeowners. Doug's work speaks to every one of our core principles. Research shows that addressing potential emergencies—even one time—can save lives and protect valuable resources. Read *Firescaping* and share it widely!"
—*Milena Fiore, executive director, ReScape California*

2nd Edition

FIRESCAPING

Protecting Your Home with a Fire-Resistant Landscape

Douglas Kent

WILDERNESS PRESS . . . *on the trail since 1967*

Firescaping: Protecting Your Home with a Fire-Resistant Landscape

1st edition 2005
2nd edition 2019
Copyright © 2005 and 2019 by Douglas Kent

Published by **WILDERNESS PRESS**
An imprint of AdventureKEEN
2204 First Ave. S, Ste. 102
Birmingham, AL 35233
800-443-7227; fax 205-326-1012

Library of Congress Cataloging-in-Publication Data

Names: Kent, Douglas (Douglas K.), author.
Title: Firescaping : protecting your home with a fire-resistant landscape / [by Douglas Kent].
Description: 2nd edition. | Birmingham, AL : Wilderness Press, 2019. | Includes bibliographical references and index.
Identifiers: LCCN 2019009783 | ISBN 9780899979625 (pbk.) | ISBN 9780899979632 (ebook)
Subjects: LCSH: Firescaping—California.
Classification: LCC SB475.9.F57 K46 2019 | DDC 635.9/509794—dc23
LC record available at https://lccn.loc.gov/2019009783

Visit wildernesspress.com for a complete listing of our books and for ordering information. Contact us at our website, at facebook.com /wildernesspress1967, or at twitter.com/wilderness1967 with questions or comments. To find out more about who we are and what we're doing, visit blog.wildernesspress.com.

Distributed by Publishers Group West
Printed in China

Front cover illustration copyright © Artazum/Shutterstock
Interior illustrations by Douglas Kent and Richard Kent
Interior photos by Douglas Kent and the following (all from Shutterstock): page 1: Alf Manciagli; page 7: Erich Fend; page 15: Steve Heap; page 17: egschiller; page 18 (top): Jenn Huls; page 18 (bottom): SpeedShutter; page 19: Yentafern; page 20: Maruoka.Joe; page 21 (bottom): strawberrytiger; page 21 (top): Juli Scalzi; page 22 (top): Karen Hermann; page 22 (bottom): Artazum; page 39: Tamara Kulikova; page 58 (top): Bob Pool; page 58 (bottom): Ranglen; page 64: Peter Turner Photography; page 66 (top): Sevennight; page 66 (bottom): Bakusova; page 68: vincent noel; page 71 (left): Nita in Wanderland; page 71 (right): mizy; page 72 (top right): Przemyslaw Muszynski; page 72 (bottom left): Nikolay Kurzenko; page 72 (bottom right): Joyce Vincent; page 76: Miao Liao; page 83: Pup Tinnarat; page 79: Oatties; page 81: Johnnie Martin; page 95: Alexander Denisenko; page 98: ArTono; page 99: maristos; page 111: Josephine Julian; page 112: Ilya Sviridenko; page 115 (bottom right): Jula Store; page 115 (top): Deyana Stefanova Robova; page 116: RebeccaJaneCall; page 118: Aleksei Zakirov; page 120: visualpower; page 129: Jason Finn; page 130: Nashepard; page 132: Gulthara; page 132: Merrimon Crawford; page 138: robert cicchetti

Cover design: Travis Bryant
Book design: Jonathan Norberg
Project editor: Kate Johnson
Proofreader: Rebecca Henderson
Indexer: Rich Carlson

TABLE OF CONTENTS

DEDICATION

Firescaping is dedicated to all the people motivated to protect themselves and others from wildfire.

It is dedicated to the diligent homeowners and community activists, the people willing to give up weekends to pull weeds or staff fire-information booths at local fairs. It is dedicated to the businesses that have been maintained to provide sanctuary during an emergency. And it is dedicated to the individuals risking their lives to protect our communities.

This book is dedicated to the people strong enough—if not bold enough—to protect their family, property, and neighbors from wildfire. If you are reading this book, *Firescaping* is dedicated to you.

ACKNOWLEDGMENTS

What started as a simple gardening guide in 1992 for a small community in northern California blossomed into a project that has traveled through the most flammable areas of the state. This work has taken me to the front lines of wildfires and in front of thousands of people.

Every step along this adventure has taught me something. I am immensely grateful for every article and book I have read, every entity that has hired me, every burned garden I have walked in, every expert who has spent time with me, and every person who has shared their story of trauma and survival.

I would like to acknowledge California's incredibly resilient and sometimes foolishly optimistic people. You won't find a harder-working bunch anywhere.

INTRODUCTION

Impassioned activists sparked my interest in fire-scaping. The Oakland/Berkeley Tunnel Fire of 1991 inspired them. Few conflagrations can compare to that one. The Tunnel Fire took 25 lives and 2,900 homes in just 10 hours. But from that firestorm sprang an incredible reaction.

State and federal interest in fire protection flourished after the Tunnel Fire. Building codes were updated. Massive grants became available for controlled burns, mechanical clearing, and greenwaste removal. And public education—whether free literature, classes, or public service announcements—became more visible and frequent. I was sure we would see a reduction of loss after the massive outpouring. I was wrong.

Since 1992, California has experienced 15 of its 20 worst fires ever—including 4 of the top 5 (based on number of structures lost). But tragedy is hardly a crazy California thing. Conflagrations are consuming more lives, structures, and acres throughout the United States. Arizona, Colorado, Florida, Idaho, Montana, Nevada, New Mexico, Oregon, Tennessee, Texas, and Washington are setting records. Americans are becoming increasingly terrorized by wildfire.

And it is not just the United States. Australia, Canada, Chile, Germany, Madagascar, Russia, Spain, sub-Saharan Africa, and even Ireland are also being overrun.

Scientists, fire professionals, and ecologists such as myself now believe the worst is still ahead. Megafires, firestorms, and fire tornados are becoming a yearly phenomenon. The two primary reasons driving the increase in ferocity and loss are well known:

1. **A warming planet:** Higher temperatures create drier, more ignitable landscapes. Warming also increases the likelihood of fire weather: exceptionally hot, windy days with low humidity have increased in frequency in recent years.

2. **More structures in fire country:** *Rural* used to mean a few hundred people living in the hills; now it means a few thousand. According to fire experts, there are more than 46 million homes representing a population of more than 100 million in high fire hazard areas in the United States. Sixty percent of all new homes are being built in fire country.

But climate change does not wholly explain the intensity of modern wildfires. People have a profound impact too. Air pollution has changed historic patterns of fire. Decades of wildfire suppression have led to enormous fuel loads. And as you will read in Chapter 2, compliance with brush-clearance laws is dismally low.

Firescaping can absolutely help you create a safer environment. This book has been designed as a series of prioritized checklists. The primary priorities are:

- Ensuring an effective rate of travel. Lives are lost when poor roads hinder both fleeing and fighting.

- Defending a home or business from an assault of flying embers—the leading cause of structure loss during a wildfire.

- Maintaining a property so that it does not spread and grow a wildfire.

- Creating safer neighborhoods through effective vegetation management.

- Quickly recovering after a wildfire passes, reducing the likelihood of soil slides, topsoil loss, and the damage that comes with both.

I hope everyone—homeowners and contractors, students and advocates—uses this book as a starting point for their journey toward personal safety. I was inspired to pursue mine by many impassioned works.

I believe that we can adapt to a changing world; that we can cultivate properties, communities, and ideas that ensure safety, resiliency, and health. Despite the frightening firestorms of recent years, we can create safety. We just need to roll up our sleeves and get to it.

Hopefully, you and I will meet in a garden.

—*Doug*

ECOLOGICAL COSTS

Wildfire has roamed throughout North America for tens of thousands of years. Renewal, diversity, and ecological health have typically flourished in its aftermath. But wildfires do not rejuvenate urbanized areas for the following reasons:

- Erosion following an urban wildfire can increase by as much as 200%. This erosion can lead to a loss of life and property.

- Local industry is shut down. Whether tourism or mining, manufacturing or retail, it takes years for a community's economic core to recover.

- Smoke heavy with particulates and carcinogens dramatically increases respiratory ailments. Burning cars, couches, and refrigerators compound these health risks.

- Rebuilding is ecologically costly. About 60 trees go into the average house, and this is along with the finite resources, such as metals, and the toxic materials, such as adhesives, preservatives, and finishes.

- Costs to battle wildfires are astronomical. Firefighting is equipment- and labor-intensive, costing taxpayers billions annually.

Letting wildfire roam in wild landscapes is often a good idea, but it cannot be allowed to run through urbanized areas. Fire-safe and firescaped communities save lives, protect economic resiliency, improve public health, preserve valuable resources, and are able to swiftly recover.

CHAPTER 1
IDENTIFYING FIRE HAZARD AREAS

More than 100 million Americans live with the risk of losing their homes to a wildfire—and that number is rapidly growing. According to land-use experts, 40% of the nation's new development is occurring in the wildland/urban interface (WUI), an innocuous seam where the flammable wildlands meld into urban features.

To help homeowners determine if their homes are at risk, the government identifies fire hazard severity zones. These areas are divided into three classes of risk: moderate, high, and very high. Classifications are made by evaluating an area's proximity to wildlands, the likelihood of those lands drying, the chance of fire weather, the type of terrain, the type and condition of the plants, the ability to mobilize evacuation and emergency responses, and the area's wildfire history.

Dense urban areas are not immune to this dangerous distinction. Scores of urban communities sit directly downwind of areas notorious for burning, and they are at risk of firebrands and inflammation.

Above: A fire hazard neighborhood

Unfortunately, our world is changing, and quickly. It is becoming hotter and drier. Areas that were impervious to fire just a couple of decades ago are now being overrun. Government-produced fire hazard maps are rarely updated more than once every five years. You may be living in a hazardous area but lack the official designation because the maps have not kept pace with the changing environment. Use the information in this chapter to evaluate your community and neighborhood.

THE NATURE OF FIRE

Fuel, heat, oxygen, conduction, convection, and *radiation:* These are the six keywords used to understand the nature of fire.

Fuel, heat, and oxygen are fire's fundamental ingredients. Without any one of them, it cannot exist. Of these, the homeowner, business owner, or governing agency manages only one—fuel.

Conduction, convection, and *radiation* are used to explain how fire spreads. Conduction moves fire by contact; convection, by rising heat; and radiation, by heat waves that radiate in every direction.

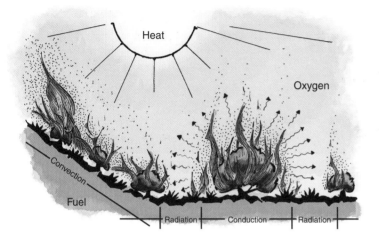

The six factors affecting the generation and spread of fire

DEFINING FIRE HAZARD AREAS

As stated, a fire hazard area is defined by proximity to wildlands, weather, terrain, vegetation, emergency access, and history. These criteria are explained below.

1. WILDLANDS

For simplicity, this book defines *wildlands* as any large plot of land that is not maintained and where the vegetation can naturally grow and reproduce. Grasslands and weedy hills, chaparral and floodplains, mixed evergreen and conifer forests, and even alpine and marshy environments are considered wildlands.

Wildlands endanger their urban neighbors only when the moisture in the plants drops to ignition levels. From the point of ignition, the weather, terrain, type of plants, and effectiveness of emergency responders determine how destructive a wildfire becomes.

FIRE HAZARD AREAS: WHAT AN OFFICIAL DESIGNATION MEANS FOR YOU

If a community has been designated as a fire hazard area, then individual property owners can expect various impacts. The most common are listed below.

Building codes: Construction projects in a fire hazard area will be subject to laws governing roads and infrastructure, placement of structures, types of setbacks, building materials, plants that can and cannot be used, and amount of vegetation clearance. The severity of these codes is typically based on the severity of the fire hazard area classification.

Real estate disclosure: Sellers of property that is within a fire hazard area might have to disclose that fact to prospective buyers.

Insurance rates: Contextually, a fire hazard area is different from an individual's personal level of risk; they are two different measures. However, insurance companies study fire hazard maps and historical fires to understand aggregate levels of risk. Classification of a fire hazard area, and its level of severity, will most likely influence your insurance rates.

Special taxes: People living in fire hazard areas might have to pay a special fee to help support fire protection services, whether that's a building or property easement or a tax.

2. WEATHER

Weather will provide the spark, fuel the fire, and then fan a conflagration across great tracts of land. It is the most dominant factor in determining whether a wildland will erupt in flames.

Wildlands surround the clustered developments pictured here, and these people live in a very high fire hazard area.

A wildfire will not start until the moisture content of the live and dead fuels on a landscape drops to ignition levels. Weather is what allows this drying to happen. If you live in an area with warm temperatures, periods of low humidity, moderate to high winds, and droughts, then you live in an area with the risk of wildfire.

Covered below are the essentials of weather in fire country: Red Flag Days and the danger of climatic extremes.

FIRE WEATHER AND RED FLAG DAYS Fire weather, often called Red Flag Days, is whipped up anytime low humidity, hot temperatures, and moderate–high winds are found together. Low humidity pulls moisture from the plants and soil, hot temperatures preheat the living and dead fuels, and winds fan any unfortunate spark.

FOEHN WINDS Foehn winds are exceptionally dangerous. They are distinguished by a rapid rise in temperature and a big drop in humidity. They are often fast, gusty, and erratic and can be found throughout the world and many parts of the US, including Alabama, Alaska, California, Colorado, Georgia, Montana, Oregon, South Carolina, Washington, and Wyoming. They are also called Chinook, devil, diablo, katabolic, Santa Ana, and sundowner winds. Foehn winds are typically generated one of three ways: the lee effect, katabolic winds, or pressure differentials.

The lee effect is produced when a strong wind runs into a mountain and drops its moisture as it is pushed upslope, eventually becoming compressed at the peak and

How a foehn (pressure differential) wind works

running down the leeside of the mountain, becoming drier and faster as it travels.

Katabolic winds are simply those that rush down a slope pushed by nothing more than gravity, gaining speed and losing moisture as they drop. Sundowners are often katabolic and occur when heat-generated breezes have been shoved up a mountain all day, only to die down at sunset and descend.

Pressure differentials are what plague California. When a high-pressure weather system sits over the Great Basin and a low-pressure system sits off the coast, the high pressure flows to the low and winds heat up, dry, and strengthen as they are shoved up and over the mountains and through the valleys and passes.

The impact of wind on probability of destruction cannot be understated. For example, dry ground cover no higher than 2 feet tall will produce 9-foot flames in 5-mph winds. That same plant will produce 19-foot flames in 20-mph winds. And that is on flat ground, meaning that flame length can exceed 75 feet on a 20% slope! (See next page for more on how slopes affect fire.)

See page 15 for important safety guidelines to follow on Red Flag Days.

CLIMATIC EXTREMES Climatic events that fall outside of average weather will alter the environment, sometimes considerably. These are the weather events that either spur unusually high rates of growth or cause sudden increases in the amount of dead material.

For the communities actively managing urban fuels, the events below should be a call to arms. The deadwood and danger these events cause must be cleaned from private property, public spaces, and roads.

DROUGHT Seasonal or prolonged drought will severely weaken plants. Drought causes excess leaf drop; prematurely kills older branches; and makes plants more susceptible to injury, pests, and ignition. Because a landscape dries earlier in the season during a drought, wildfire season starts earlier as well. Fuel-reduction efforts must be doubled during droughts.

FREEZES Freezes and prolonged frosts can cause widespread damage in poorly adapted communities. Killing plants and limbs, these unusually low temperatures create an enormous amount of deadwood in just a couple of days. Injured plants, if they are not pruned, also become more susceptible to the effects of heat, pests, and wind, creating even more deadwood in the years following the initial injury. In fact, many experts claim that an unusually hard freeze in the winter of 1991 contributed to the ferocity of the Tunnel Fire nine months later (it took 25 lives and consumed 2,900 structures in just 10 hours).

Freeze damage and deadwood

3. TERRAIN

Differences in terrain explain why some areas are more fire prone than others, despite experiencing the same type of weather. Slopes, canyons, and ridgetops are notoriously fire prone and dangerous. And while flat ground is the safest terrain by far, even that is dicey during fire weather, as many Northern California communities can attest.

Covered below are the three riskiest places to live: on slopes, in canyons and valleys, and atop ridges.

SLOPES Wildfires on slopes burn hotter, run faster, and produce longer flames than fires on flat ground. For every 10% increase in slope, the length of flame will double, meaning that if a grassy ground fire produces 6-foot flames, they will lengthen to 24 feet on a 20% slope—more than enough to jump up and into houses and trees. Additionally, the soils on slopes typically dry before those on flat ground, making the plants more ignitable as well.

Slopes are dangerous for another reason: they are more expensive to maintain and receive less maintenance as a consequence. Labor costs are high, time-saving big machines are often impractical, going up and down takes longer, and the risk of personal injury is greater.

CANYONS AND VALLEYS Winds become compressed and stronger when pushed through narrow areas, making canyons and valleys particularly fire prone. Many of the nation's most horrific fires have originated in and devoured canyons. Firefighters typically battle a blaze at the top of these great depressions, making the homes midslope defenseless and vulnerable.

Winds are stronger in canyons and valleys because of a phenomenon called the Venturi effect. This effect is the same as putting your thumb over a hose to get it to shoot farther; the water or wind rushes through compressions to maintain equilibrium on either side. Some of the places prone to the Venturi effect are canyons, gorges, passes, ravines, saddles, trenches, and valleys.

RIDGETOPS Properties along the top of a slope are probably the most dangerous. Wildfires can come from any direction, and firebrands will be ever present. Ridgetop property owners must expect to play a pivotal role in helping firefighters battle a blaze, or they risk being completely isolated from community resources and being expected to battle the blaze on their own.

If the local fire agency has designated your ridgetop as a place to fight a fire, then there will be strict and diligent enforcement of fire codes. If the ridgetop is too dangerous for emergency personnel, then you will need to be

A dangerous canyon

A dangerous ridgetop

able to defend yourself, which would include having large caches of stored water, a separate power supply (generators or batteries), water pumps, fire hoses, many escape routes, and reliable communication links. Refer to Chapter 12 ("Ridgetop and Understory Properties") for more details.

4. TYPE OF VEGETATION

Any landscape that dries to the point of easy ignition is a fire hazard. But what happens after the landscape is ablaze determines its fire hazard ranking.

Vegetation is evaluated using three measures: what are the chances of ignition, how long will it sustain a fire, and how much heat does it produce when ablaze? These three measures are called: ignitability, sustainability, and combustibility.

Ignitability is determined by measuring the time it takes a plant to burst into flames when exposed to grass or forest fire temperatures, roughly between 650°F and 1,100°F. A plant's leaf-moisture content and thickness directly affect the amount of time it takes to ignite. Dry savanna is highly ignitable, whereas north-facing chaparral is much less so.

Sustainability is defined by the amount of time a plant or landscape can sustain a fire. Sustainability is determined by the amount of dry fuel. Scrub, for instance, quickly exhausts its fuels, whereas conifer forests can sustain a fire for days.

Combustibility is defined by the amount of heat a plant or landscape produces when inflamed. The greater the heat, the greater the thermal radiation and wind—and the greater a fire's spread. Amount and density of the dry fuels determines the combustibility of a plant or landscape.

Grasslands, for example, have high ignitability and burn at greater frequencies but have low sustainability and combustibility, meaning that they are easier to extinguish. Conversely, a mixed-evergreen forest has low ignitability but high sustainability and combustibility, meaning that it may not ignite for decades but produces devastating results when it does because of its intense heat and difficulty in extinguishing.

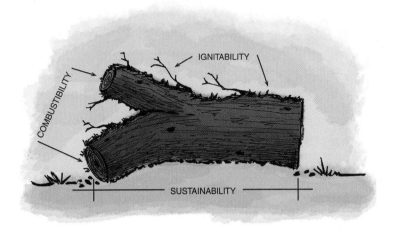

Every plant has different levels of ignitability, combustibility, and sustainability.

However, your home does not care if the sparks raining on it come from a grass fire or a forest fire—it only takes one firebrand to take down a house. Your home, business, and community must be prepared regardless of the surrounding landscape. People tend to be more vigilant in areas with frequent fires and more complacent in areas that have not seen a significant fire in decades. Consequently, a majority of the most recent and destructive wildfires have occurred in forested areas.

5. EMERGENCY RESPONSE

Access is fundamental to saving lives and properties. The ability of firefighters to combat a fire influences an area's fire hazard ranking. You may live on flat ground and be surrounded by perennial grasses (a moderate fire hazard), but if emergency personnel cannot access the area due to terrain or remoteness, then you live in a high fire hazard area.

6. HISTORY

In the past, the first step in determining an area's fire hazard ranking was looking at historical fire maps. The thinking was that if a community had been overrun by wildfire before, then it was a sure bet that a conflagration would roar through it again; conversely, if there were no fires in recorded history, then the probability would be very low. Unfortunately, that simple methodology does not work as well anymore.

Our planet is warming, and many parts of our continent are becoming hotter and drier. Areas that were once impervious to wildfires are now being consumed by them. Please, go back through this chapter and truly evaluate your community's weather, its terrain, and the type of vegetation found there, and develop your own opinion. History is no longer the most reliable indicator of wildfire hazard.

YOUR LEVEL OF RISK

This chapter has defined a high fire hazard area, but it did not define your individual level of risk. If you have determined that your community is in a fire hazard area, then you need to answer three additional questions:

1. Can you safely and swiftly evacuate?

2. Will your house or business survive the eventual firestorm?

3. Is your property in danger of being overrun by a debris flow following a wildfire?

This book's mission is to help you answer and address these fundamental questions.

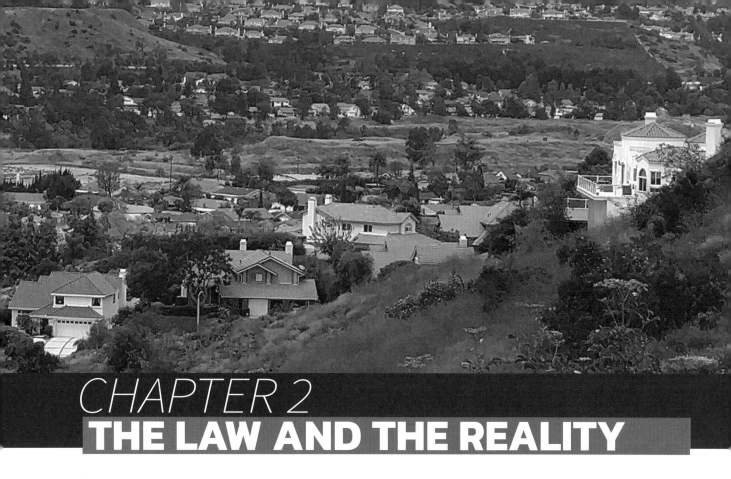

CHAPTER 2
THE LAW AND THE REALITY

As the country's population and temperatures increase, so do the laws and obligations aimed at fire safety. *Rural* used to mean a couple hundred people living in the woods; now it means a couple thousand. There is more to lose in our flammable mountains, foothills, and valleys than ever before.

Knowing the laws around fire protection is fundamental. If you live in an area with high danger and strict enforcement, noncompliance can lead to citations and even property liens. However, most people do not live in those types of neighborhoods, and the reality of compliance is often much different from the law.

Above: Living harmoniously in fire country is no easy task. Wildfires, erosion, and pests must be negotiated, along with the laws and expectations of the community. **Top:** This community has survived three brushfires in the last 15 years. Defensible space, strong architecture, and consistent maintenance have allowed the residents to live alongside fire.

THE LAW

The federal government actively provides and supports model laws and standards for vegetation management in fire hazard areas. However, it does not impose laws on private property. The laws pertaining to property management are overseen by state, county, city, and community-association ordinances.

A fire hazard area is any property, neighborhood, or community that adjoins mountainous, forested, or brush- or grass-covered areas. Fire agencies designate fire hazard areas by examining topography, vegetation type, and likelihood of fire weather. If a property is in an area designated with a moderate or high risk of fire, then local fire agencies will probably want to impose these minimum requirements:

EVACUATION ROUTES

- Clearance of flammable fuels is mandatory, although the amount required varies. Some agencies require 10 feet of clearance; others, 50 feet.

- Wild vegetation must be mowed to 18 inches on either side of the route.

STRUCTURES

- The roof must be Class A, the most fire resistant.

- A noncombustible sheet must sit between the roof tiles and the plywood.

- Air vents (ventilation openings) are screened with ⅛-inch mesh that is both noncombustible and corrosion resistant. Agencies in extra-high fire risk areas may require 1⁄16-inch screens.

- Siding and the undersides of eaves and soffits must be constructed of no less than ignition-resistant material. Noncombustible is always preferred.

- Exterior windows must be glazed and double-paned.

- Doors and other openings must be constructed of ignition-resistant materials.

- Chimney outlets must have a screen.

- Portions of a structure that overhang a slope must be skirted to grade with no less than ignition-resistant materials.

DEFENSIBLE SPACE

- A firebreak must be maintained at least 30 or 50 feet around a structure or property line, whichever is closest.

- Landscape features, such as decks and shade structures, must be constructed from ignition-resistant materials. Noncombustible building materials, such as metal and stone, may be required in extra-high fire hazard areas.

- Trees next to a structure must be kept clear of deadwood.

- Wild vegetation must be mowed to 18 inches.

Some properties and communities fall into a category called extra-high fire hazard area. Generally, this designation is assigned because of the type of vegetation, the topography, and the likelihood of experiencing fire weather. However, some neighborhoods might earn this classification because of insufficient water supplies, inadequate emergency-response resources or extended response times, limited accessibility, or dangerous terrain.

If a property falls within an extra-high fire hazard area, then the amount of defensible space that must be maintained from a structure grows to 100 or 200 feet. These properties may also have to construct off-street parking, greenbelts, no-ignition areas for machine work, and an emergency supply of water.

ENFORCEMENT

If a property falls into a category of high to extra-high fire hazard area, then fire codes will be more demanding and enforcement likely. A property that falls in a high fire hazard area must maintain some degree of clearance. Should property owners fail to maintain fire safety, then they become subject to citation and fines. If an owner remains remiss, an overseeing agency, typically the local fire department, can contract to have the work done, seeking payment in court, oftentimes resulting in a property lien.

People working to create safer environments in fire country must address the four primary reasons people are resistant to making fire protection a way of life, described below.

THE EXPENSE OF FIRE PROTECTION

Wildfires are completely natural in wild areas, and one of the surest ways to protect a home is to clear excess fuels. After the 2003 Cedar Fire in San Diego County, in which 15 people died and 2,820 buildings were destroyed, the *Los Angeles Times* reported that 90% of the surviving homes had just 30 feet of defensible space.

The importance of defensible space cannot be understated. Nineteen elite firefighters died while battling a wildfire in Yarnell, Arizona, in 2013. These firefighters were helping protect about 600 structures, yet only 63 of those (just over 10%) were properly protected. Experts

throughout the nation's fire hazard areas claim that compliance with brush clearance ordinances ranges from 3% to 25%. Clearing land of flammable fuels is an exception, not the rule.

People living in fire country know the dangers—lack of compliance is not lack of understanding or a bad case of denial—people generally accept the risk, but simply fail to take action. After 20-plus years of working in fire country, I have come up with four reasons why compliance with fire codes is low.

1. **Financial expense:** Clearing land of unwanted fuels demands labor and equipment, both of which are expensive. String trimmers, chainsaws, chippers, big trucks, and the people who can wield these tools are needed to cut and haul thousands of pounds of debris. Costs to clear can exceed $4,000 an acre.

2. **Emotional expense:** Emotional fortitude is needed to remove oak saplings, mow quail habitat, and remove a mass of shrubs sheltering a herd of wrens. People in fire country generally admire, respect, and support nature, making intentionally harming habitat personally and emotionally difficult.

3. **Social expense:** Along with personal obstacles, there are also social consequences to clearing land of excess fuels. By degrees, every neighborhood has its own identity. Removing a strand of old trees can be viewed as an insult to that identity and, as I can attest, can lead to drive-by fingers and face-to-face confrontations. Conforming to the norms of some communities can increase plant fuels.

4. **Process risk:** Humans have evolved to process and act on the greatest danger

first. Fire is an ever-present danger, but not one with immediate consequences. As a result, taking action to reduce fire risk falls by the wayside in favor of solving everyday problems, such as getting the kids to school, being productive at work, or making contributions to social groups, that can be perceived as greater emergencies than fire protection.

A community committed to fire safety will have to overcome these four barriers to ensure communitywide fire protection. Communities can reduce the cost of vegetation management by providing free greenwaste disposal or free chipper use, or by organizing volunteers to help clear landscapes for residents who do not have the means to do it themselves.

Providing public education can reduce the emotional and social expense of clearing flammable vegetation. Biologists, ecologists, and horticulturists can use articles, brochures, booklets, presentations, and workshops to help property managers maintain ecological health and fire protection.

Clustered development with poor maintenance

CHAPTER 3
PROTECTING YOURSELF FROM YOURSELF

Creating a property that can withstand a conflagration is vital in fire country, but that alone may not save your home. People are far more likely to burn their own home than be overrun by a wildfire.

The leading cause of home fires in America is cooking equipment, followed by heating, electrical, accidental ignition, children playing with fire, smoking, wildfires, and then candles. While all those sources deserve a chapter, this book's focus is on wildfires.

Well over 80% of the nation's wildfires have human origins, and a majority of those are started in a landscape. Whether the origin is a burn pile escaping or a rogue campfire, an errant cigarette or equipment use, people enjoying and working in landscapes are a common and constant cause of wildfires.

This chapter explains how to manage the heat and sparks of equipment use, how to safely burn piles of vegetation, and how to keep ignition areas safe.

FIRE WEATHER AWARENESS

If your neighborhood is experiencing fire weather, a Red Flag Day, or strong dry winds, then:

- Avoid open burning, which includes piles of debris and campfires.

- Avoid outdoor barbecuing.

- Avoid the use of outdoor equipment, such as chainsaws, welding equipment, and scrappers.

- Ensure that smokers do so in an open and cleared environment that has access to water.

For a definition of fire weather and Red Flag Days, refer to Chapter 1 ("Identifying Fire Hazard Areas").

Above: Follow the guidelines in this chapter to help reduce the risk of fire—especially on days when the risk of fire is high.

LANDSCAPE EQUIPMENT

One of the most common and persistent causes of wildfires is equipment use. Mowers, string trimmers, and chainsaws are a source of friction, heat, and sparks. To avoid starting a fire while working with machinery, take the following precautions:

- Put spark arresters on all exhaust ports, and repair holes in existing systems and arresters.

- Check for a buildup of carbon in the exhaust system and on spark plugs.

- Refuel only when engine has cooled.

- Never lay a running or hot engine in grass or other ignitable vegetation.

- Bring a fire extinguisher to the work site.

- Avoid working past 10 a.m. during fire season.

- Avoid all work that involves machinery during extreme fire weather conditions: hot, dry, windy days.

Essentials for ensuring fire safety: a fire extinguisher, a board on which to lay hot equipment, and a nonspill gas container

BURNING PILES OF DEBRIS

Did you know that you could be held liable for all damages and costs of suppression if a burn pile you created started a wildfire? Not many people do. Escaping burn piles are a common cause of wildfires. Burning debris can put your neighbors and community at risk, and the task should not be taken lightly.

Some jurisdictions may require a landowner to get a burn permit before igniting a pile. Many will allow burning only during specific weather conditions or certain times of the year. Always check with your local air-quality board or fire department, and make sure there are no restrictions before burning. Follow the recommendations below for a safe and successful burn.

- *Important:* Never, ever burn debris during fire weather, during periods of high wind, or when wind is predicted.

- Never burn a pile bigger than 4 feet high and wide.

- Keep piles of debris separated by 20 feet or more.

- Clear flammable material and vegetation 10 feet around the debris pile.

- Make sure you have vertical clearance and that nothing flammable, such as tree limbs or power lines, is above the pile.

- Keep a fire extinguisher on hand, as well as a bucket of water and shovels.

- Never leave a burn unattended.

- Burn only vegetation—never household garbage or petroleum-based materials, such as plastics, plywood, or rubber.

- Always extinguish the fire before leaving. Soak the pile and turn it over several times with a shovel.

- Visit the pile several hours after it was extinguished to make sure that it is out.

IGNITION AREAS

There are areas within a landscape that routinely produce sparks and fires. These areas include barbecues, fire pits, roads, smoking spaces, and work areas. Follow the brief guidelines below to help protect yourself. For more on designing and maintaining ignition areas, refer to Chapters 9, 14, 16, and 17.

- Vigilantly remove dead, dying, and diseased vegetation around areas of possible ignition.

- Remove limbs no less than 10 feet above these areas, including barbecues and chimneys.

- Install spark arresters on all chimneys and small engines, such as gasoline-powered well pumps.

- Use and maintain Zone 1 plants, which are the most fire resistant (for more on Zone Theory, see Chapter 9, page 42).

- Use the most fire-resistant material, such as metal and stone, for constructed features, such as posts and walls.

A proper burn pile, like this one, should be no more than 4 feet high and wide and separated from other piles by 20 feet or more.

CHAPTER 4
WHAT TO DO DURING A FIRE

Humans, as a rule, are not the sharpest thinkers in emergencies. We tend to wait too long to take action, we underestimate the severity of an emergency, we overestimate our abilities, or, worst, we are simply unprepared for the inevitable emergency. A majority of the lives lost in wildfires are due to spontaneous and unplanned evacuations.

Below is hardened advice on how to prioritize your time during a wildfire and mandatory evacuation. Hopefully it will help you save yourself, your loved ones, and your valuables.

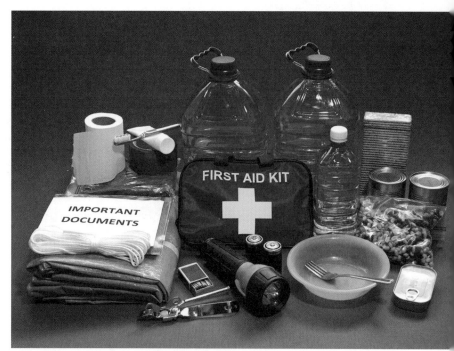

Above: Prepack an emergency supply kit that you can grab in a hurry. **Top:** Don't wait for an evacuation order. Fires can move quickly and erratically, and leaving sooner can put you at an advantage if many families are on the roads.

Do not panic. Breathe and follow the steps in this chapter in an emergency.

1. PROTECT YOURSELF AND OTHERS

- **Park** cars off driveways and roadways, ensuring that emergency vehicles can get by. Roll up windows, and leave the keys in the ignition.

- **Wear** wool or cotton pants, a long-sleeved shirt, and a jacket.

- **Grab** a pair of gloves, a handkerchief (which can be used wet as a mask), and several bottles of drinking water for each person in your group.

- **Pack** irreplaceable items, such as laptops, photographs, art, address books, bonds, stocks, and birth certificates.

- **Pack** everything you'll need for a couple of days away from home, such as medications, toiletries, and a change of clothes.

- **Fill** extra bottles of drinking water. This can make a huge difference in an emergency.

BREATHING EASIER IN WILDFIRES

Breathing smoke from wildfires is not only painful but also harmful. It is heavy with noxious gases, particulates, and carcinogens. People in areas affected by wildfires can expect to experience some type of respiratory ailment, such as difficulty breathing, bronchitis, asthma, allergies, sore airways, or exacerbation of heart and lung disease. Follow these guidelines to protect your airway and lungs:

- **Stay indoors.** Keep doors and windows closed, and avoid lighting candles, making fires, vacuuming, and any other activity that increases indoor dust.

- **Avoid common paper dust masks.** They are designed to block large particles, like sawdust, and not the fine particles that cause the most respiratory damage. Furthermore, they rarely provide a snug fit and may actually trap the most dangerous particulates behind the mask.

The minimum type of mask needed for wildfires is an N95 mask. These masks are better fitting than paper and are rated to filter 95% of very small (0.3-micron) particles. They do not work as well on people with facial hair, however.

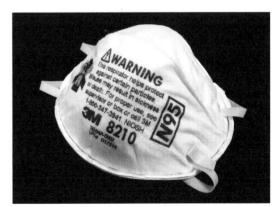

An N95 mask is easy to find, simple to use, and the most common mask for smoke-choked areas.

The best device for breathing outside in heavy smoke is what the firefighters commonly use: the self-contained breathing apparatus (SCBA). While this gear supplies canned oxygen and clean air, it is heavy (30-plus pounds), needs training to use, and usually lasts only an hour.

Breathing through a moistened handkerchief, shirt, or towel does not provide much protection against gases and particulates, but it is better than nothing. Furthermore, the moisture can cool and humidify the air you breathe, making it less painful. Try to breathe through your nose.

2. PROTECT YOUR PAPERS

If you live in an area prone to wildfires, then the following papers should be kept together and in a transportable carrying case:

- Insurance polices
- Deed/mortgage papers
- Birth and death certificates
- Social security cards (numbers)
- Passports
- Three years of tax returns
- Will and trust documents
- Titles to vehicles
- Professional licenses/certificates
- Medical information
- Medical insurance cards
- Bank account numbers
- A complete household inventory

3. PROTECT THE INSIDE OF YOUR HOME

- **First:** Make sure the gas is turned off at the line leading to the house.

- **Close all doors and windows** inside the house; attic, basement, and eave vents; blinds and other nonflammable window coverings.

- **Remove fabric drapes** from windows.

- **Turn on all lights** inside a home or structure.

- **Turn off fans** and heating and cooling systems.

- **Fill bathtubs and sinks with water.**

- **Unlock all doors** when you leave. In the fires of 2003, one fireman was seriously injured and another died trying to get into and defend a house that was locked.

Before evacuating, fill containers such as bathtubs and outdoor trash cans with water.

Above: If you cannot take your pet with you, be sure to leave it untethered. **Below:** A sticker like this tells responders to search your house for pets and drop them off at a pet-friendly evacuation center.

4. PROTECT YOUR PETS

Pets have three options during a fire: flee with you, stay in a safe place while you fight the fire, or get left behind as you flee. You can take steps to increase the chances of your pet's survival in each situation.

- **First:** Make sure the animal has an identification tag, even if that means writing your phone number on their coat.

- **Second:** Grab a photo of your pet for identification purposes.

- **Pack** a week's worth of pet food and medicine.

- **Secure:** If you decide to fight the fire, place your pet in a familiar and safe spot, such as your car.

- **Untether:** If for any reason you have to flee without taking your pet, uncage or untie it.

- **Prearrange** a network of community resources, family, friends, and some hotels where you can safely leave your animals. Hop online and see if your city has emergency shelters for animals.

In Case of
EMERGENCY
Please Save Our Pets

Dog's Name: _____
Cat's Name: _____
Others: _____

5. PROTECT THE OUTSIDE OF YOUR HOME

- **Remove combustible materials** from under and around the house. These include newspaper, firewood, furniture, and plants that have grown up and under a house.

- **Lean ladders** against the side of the house, creating easy access to the roof.

- **Sweep roof** to remove ignitable material.

- **Eliminate flammable features** and obstacles such as patio furniture by putting them inside the house or placing them farther away.

- **Attach hoses to faucets.** If possible, screw an adjustable nozzle onto the end of each hose.

- **Place shovels,** rakes, hoes, and other tools that might be useful in a visible location.

- **Fill large trash cans** and buckets with water, and place around the structure.

- **Water** flammable roofs, landscape features, and the garden.

Above: Lean ladders against the exterior of your house to allow easy access to the roof. **Below:** Clear furniture and other clutter from around your house to reduce fuels and clear the path for emergency responders.

FIRESCAPING

CHAPTER 5
PRIORITIZING YOUR TIME

The area where you live has been designated a fire hazard severity zone, but that does little to inform you of the real risks you must overcome on your property; it does little to help you prioritize your time and money to ensure your family's safety. Covered below are the six priorities that help ensure safety in fire country. Once you have checked one box, move on to the next.

Determining the chance that life or property will be lost due to a wildfire is complicated. It is influenced not only by your house's ability to withstand firebrands but also by your landscape's ability to slow or stop the fire, your ability to flee quickly, and your community's ability to respond effectively to a wildfire. Below is a list of the basics of preparing for wildfires.

1. **HAVE AN EVACUATION PLAN** First and foremost, take care of these items, which prioritize your personal safety and basic needs, before moving on to the others. For more discussion, refer to Chapter 3 ("Protecting Yourself from Yourself") and Chapter 16 ("Maintenance Priorities").

- Make sure every driver in your household knows the evacuation routes.

- Categorize and centralize your most valuable possessions.

- Develop an evacuation plan for your pets.

Above: Overview of the six aspects of emergency preparedness, covered in this chapter. **Top:** A narrow road with dense vegetation and overhanging branches will impede firefighters' ability to access your home.

- Make sure you have stored water, food, batteries, phone chargers, flashlights, blankets, and toilet paper.

- Make sure everyone in your household has a fire outfit: durable, tough shoes; sturdy long pants; wool long-sleeved shirt; leather (not plastic) gloves; and safety goggles.

2. CLEAR ENTRANCE AND EXIT ROUTES. Your ability to swiftly evacuate and firefighters' ability to quickly enter are vital to protecting life and property. Below are the basics. For more discussion on designing and maintaining a property and community that can accommodate both fleeing and fighting, refer to Chapter 4 ("What To Do During a Fire"), Chapter 6 ("Roads"), Chapter 9 ("The Zone Theory"), Chapter 17 ("Maintaining Zones 1 and 2"), and Chapter 21 ("Community Obligations").

- Clear the road leading to your house of flammable vegetation.

- Make sure your house number is visible from the street.

- Clear your driveway of flammable vegetation, and have ample room for a truck to turn around.

- Make sure the paths leading around your property are wide, stable, and easy to navigate.

- Make sure the first 30 feet around your house is cleared of dead, dying, and diseased vegetation.

3. PREPARE YOUR STRUCTURE. It's more likely for a firebrand (wind-propelled ember) to ignite some flammable element of your home and destroy it than for your house to be overrun by direct flame contact. Creating a home that can withstand a barrage that might last for days is paramount. For more discussion, refer to Chapter 7 ("Structures") and Chapter 16 ("Maintenance Priorities").

- Make sure your roof is Class A and free of ignitable debris during fire season.

- Ensure that all vents and entry points into a structure are either properly sealed or screened.

- Repair any blemishes to the siding, such as peeling paint, split wood, or widening joints.

- Remove tree limbs hanging 10 feet or less above the roof.

- Ensure that any architectural or landscape feature that overhangs a slope is either skirted or properly defended.

- Remove anything remotely flammable from within 5 feet of your house. This includes debris, furniture, and poor plants.

4. ESTABLISH DEFENSIBLE SPACE. Firebrands and heat are actively beaten back in Zone 1, defensible space. This is the area that will protect not only your house but also the people trying to defend it. Below are the basics of protection, but for more detailed design and maintenance guides, refer to Chapters 9–18.

- Remove anything remotely flammable from within 5 feet of the house.

- Remove all dead, dying, and diseased vegetation.

- Irrigate plants just before signs of water stress.

- Maintain stable, wide, and easy-to-navigate paths.

- Maintain large and safe areas where firefighters can work.

5. MAINTAIN OUTLYING AREAS. Not only does the condition of outlying areas affect the chances of your house surviving, but it also affects your neighborhood's chances of survival. Your outlying areas can either slow a fire or help it spread. For more discussion, refer to Chapter 9 ("The Zone Theory"), Chapter 16 ("Maintenance Priorities"), and Chapter 18 ("Managing Wild Vegetation and Weeds").

- Constantly remove dead, dying, and diseased vegetation.

- Carefully manage erosion and topsoil loss.

- Create and maintain community pathways and evacuation routes.

6. **HELP YOUR COMMUNITY.** The decisions a community makes and the resources it allocates to safety have a profound impact on that community's ability to weather and recover from a conflagration. Communities need to acknowledge their risk—even if that comes with economic consequence—and then allocate the resources needed to both remedy the physical problems and inspire citizens to take action. For more discussion, refer to Chapter 6 ("Roads") and Chapter 21 ("Community Obligations").

- Help your community reduce fuels in parks, along roads, and on properties that have been vacated.

- Advocate for building-code and vegetation-clearance compliance.

- Support endeavors that would improve emergency communications.

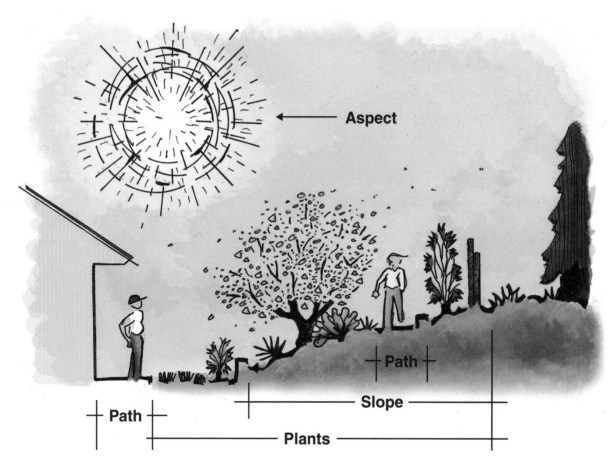

This landscape could do much better at protecting the occupants. The plants are growing a little too close together, and there is a slope, which is dangerous. The lower path is safe, but the upper is constricted and unsafe in dangerous situations.

These manzanita shrubs/trees are within 50 feet of a structure. They are also old, are growing into each other, and have twiggy interiors. This grove has the potential to catch, sustain, and propel a wildfire. It needs to be thinned and regeneration encouraged.

- Join and support organizations that help with fuel modification, evacuation, and community preparedness.

- Inspire your neighbors to reduce their fuels and threats.

Reducing Chances of Debris Flows Following a Fire

If you live in fire country, then you need to prepare as much for a fire as you do for the deadly consequences that follow—namely erosion, topsoil loss, and debris and mud flows. For more discussion on these topics, please refer to Chapter 19 ("First Aid for Fire Scarred Landscapes") and Chapter 20 ("Holding Your Hill: Long-Term Strategies").

- Clean all debris from drainage systems, which may include catch basins, culverts, ditches, roof and street gutters, and swales.

- Direct sheeting water away from injured landscapes.

- Employ mechanical devices, such as jute netting, if erosion risk is deemed high.

- Lightly water burned landscape, if dry, to inspire the germination of stored seeds—even weeds.

- Test your levels of risk and develop a long-term plan to control erosion.

CHAPTER 6
ROADS

The importance of roads cannot be overstated. Surviving an urban conflagration involves both fleeing and fighting, and both demand roads that can allow for two-way traffic and easy navigation during periods of poor visibility. Not only do roads provide access, but they are also commonly used as staging areas for fighting a fire. Below are the design and maintenance characteristics of a good road in fire country.

ROAD WIDTH

Nineteen of the 25 people killed in the Tunnel Fire (Oakland/Berkeley, 1991) were trapped in their cars. Nine of those 19 were caught on Charing Cross Road, a small, winding ribbon that was built in the 1920s and measured no more than 14 feet wide. The national requirement for two-lane road width is 27 feet. Two people died trying to get on Charing Cross from their driveways, and the other 8, only a few blocks away on similar roads.

Above: Will the road in front of your house lead to safety? The road pictured above looks dangerous. **Top:** This single-lane road offers a pullout, which helps prevent bottlenecks during an evacuation.

CAN YOUR ROADS HANDLE A MASS EVACUATION?

Good roads will enable safe and swift passage for both fleeing residents and incoming emergency personnel. The core factors that determine a road's safety are its width, amount of vegetation clearance, and visibility. Identify the attributes below that best describe your local roads.

ATTRIBUTES	RATING	NOTES
LOCAL ROAD (ROAD IN FRONT OF HOUSE)		
Single-lane, narrow, and curvy	Lethal	One vehicular mishap and these roads shut down.
Single-lane and curvy with some pullouts	Dangerous	Disabled, parked, or waiting cars have a place to go, ensuring flow.
Two-lane	Safe	Often these roads are turned into two lanes one way, ensuring speed.
COLLECTOR STREET (ROAD LEADING TO A CITY OR HIGHWAY)		
Single-lane, narrow, and curvy	Lethal	When multiple local roads empty to a small collector, gridlock is certain.
Single-lane with some pullouts	Dangerous	Depending on volume, these roads can either impede emergency access or enable it.
Two-lane with good forward visibility	Safe	Professionals can get in and residents can get out.
ALL ROADS AND STREETS		
Dense and dry vegetation within 10 ft. on both sides	Lethal	Flames leaping at and licking cars is not uncommon on roads like these.
Overhanging branches of flammable plants	Lethal	Ground fires travel across roads with fuel bridges like these.
Sight lines less than 100 ft.	Dangerous	Visibility falls during fires, and when poor sight lines are added, rate of travel is greatly reduced.
Narrow without a pullout for large trailer trucks every few miles	Dangerous	Large and small commercial trucks can impede rapid evacuation.
No streetlights	Bad	Visibility perilously drops in wildfires, and street-lights greatly improve rates of travel.
Two-lane, cleared vegetation, and good sight lines	Safe	These roads encourage steady rates of safe travel.

The letters in this illustration correspond to the Road Design Checklist below. These are the characteristics that enable successful flight and fight.

ROAD DESIGN CHECKLIST

No one expects homeowners to design and maintain the road that leads to their house, but that does not mean they should not be aware of the characteristics of a safe road; it is the homeowner's life and property that are at stake. If the road in front of your house lacks some of the attributes below, take action—either make a change or demand one.

A: ROAD WIDTH

Proper road width invites emergency personnel. A fire truck will be reluctant to travel down a long, narrow road if residents are still evacuating. The national standard width for a two-lane road is 27 feet, although winding hillside roads might be as narrow as 22 feet.

B: ROAD SIGNS

Road signs must be clearly visible in times of reduced visibility, heightened vulnerability, and traffic traveling at a high rate of speed. A good sign will have high contrast between the sign's background and lettering (technically, no less than 70%). Road signs are generally at least 7 feet above the height of the curb. On unpaved roads, signs might be as low as 5 feet due to the slower driving speeds. The sign itself should be no less than 12 inches tall with lettering no less than 6 inches tall. Additionally, road signs must be constructed from nonflammable materials.

C: VEGETATION

Keep flammable vegetation at least 10 feet from both sides of the road. For a list of flammable plants, refer to Chapter 13 ("Plant Selection and Fire Protection"). Keep natural vegetation that dries in summer and fall, such as grasses, forbs, and perennials, mowed to 6 inches.

D: ADDRESS

The home address should be visible from the street and from as many angles as possible. Emergency personnel may need to locate a specific structure, and stopping or slowing at each driveway to read the address can greatly hamper an effective response. The numbers should be at least 6 inches tall and be in sharp contrast to the color of the structure.

E: PULLOUTS

When cars cannot pull out of the way of fire trucks, bottlenecks will ensue, with lethal consequences. Any road that is narrower than 18 feet wide must have pullouts or off-street parking at regular intervals. Generally, a pullout or parking spot is no less than 17 feet long and 8 feet wide.

Managing overreaching trees along small roads is complicated. On one hand, they can easily transmit a fire across a fuel break, shutting down a vital artery and ultimately endangering lives. On the other hand, studies have shown these types of trees cause drivers to slow down, ultimately saving lives. Pictured above is a gorgeous but dangerous road with fire scars.

F: SIGHT LINES

Drivers must have clear lines of sight. The goal is to create no less than 155 feet of forward visibility, which is the national standard for cars traveling at 25 mph. Visibility around curves is also critical. Ideally trees and large shrubs are set back from the inside of curves.

G. LARGE VEGETATION

The trees and larger shrubs along a road should be planted and managed to enhance long sight lines, create variety and interest (slowing drivers), and force views along curves. There must be a 10-foot gap between the growing tips of trees and large shrubs. Twenty feet is far better in wooded, wild, and hillside areas.

H: DEAD ENDS

Streets that dead-end must have a place for large trucks and emergency responders to turn around. Turnarounds are often where firefighters stage an attack.

If a turnaround has not been designed for street parking, then do not allow cars to park there; if the turnaround is cluttered and difficult to navigate, firefighters will choose a more suitable location to stage a successful defense.

What are the sight lines within your community? Can you see far enough ahead to keep traffic moving during an emergency?

I: MOUNTABLE CURBS

Rolling, or mountable, curbs are essential on narrow roads. They allow large trucks to drive up them, turn around, and retreat from a dangerous situation. Although mountable curbs are more expensive to install (and that is the reason they are not more widespread), progressive cities are demanding them for all new development in high fire hazard areas.

J: EMERGENCY WATER MARKERS

Local fire agencies may issue blue reflective markers to homeowners who manage enough water to assist in firefighting. These markers must be properly placed; they should be visible from at least 155 feet away in each direction along the road. For more on emergency water supplies and systems, refer to Chapter 15.

K: GUIDE MARKERS

Guide markers help people navigate winding roads. Driving in dense smoke at night can reduce forward visibility to just 30 feet. Markers help maintain a decent rate of travel. Markers are generally reflective yellow and vary widely in design, from skinny signs no higher than 3 feet to reflectors embedded in the road.

L: ACCENTUATED FIRE HYDRANTS

Hydrants are often tough to spot in the best of situations, tougher during the night under the haze of dense ash and smoke. Whether with a streetlight, reflective markers, or cleared vegetation and bright paint, fire hydrants must be easily seen along all roads in fire country.

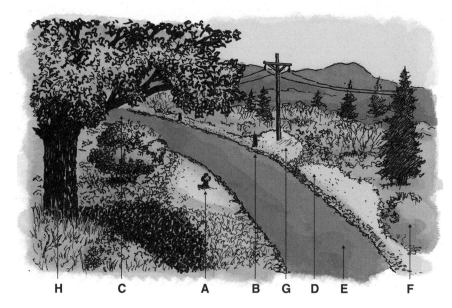

The letters in this illustration correspond to the Road Maintenance Checklist below.

ROAD MAINTENANCE CHECKLIST

Like everything, roads need care. Road capacity, rates of travel, and emergency response times are all affected by road conditions. A poorly maintained road will reduce all three. Use the checklist below to properly budget the resources and time to maintain efficient access.

A: FIRE HYDRANTS

Fire hydrants must be maintained with 3 feet of clearance around their circumference and 5 feet of mowed space in front of them.

B: GUIDE MARKERS

Roadway guide markers need good visibility to work, and vegetation should be mowed at least 2 feet around them. Ideally, the markers should be made from non-flammable materials, like metal.

C: CHECK FORWARD VISIBILITY

A visibility analysis needs to be performed every other year. The goal is to identify vegetation or objects that obstruct sight lines on roads. Mow, prune, or remove the obstructions. If the obstructions are not on your property and the risk they pose is great, then write a letter to the owner, copying the fire agency responsible for compliance. People driving at residential speeds should have at least 155 feet of forward visibility. As an ideal, people waiting at an intersection or pulling out of a driveway should have 155 feet of visibility in either direction as well.

D: ROAD SHOULDERS

The shoulders of roads should be kept clear of ignitable fuels. Some of the ways to manage shoulders are to spread gravel; flame weeds in late spring; apply herbicides or vinegar in early to midsummer; and mow vegetation at least twice a year—once in late winter/early spring to reduce the amount of weed seed, and again in late spring/early summer to reduce and remove the fine ignitable fuels.

E: RURAL DRIVING SURFACES

Gravel or dirt roads need yearly maintenance. Potholes, ruts, rills, and gullies can quickly develop and grow. These distortions greatly reduce travel speeds. Some of the yearly tasks include importing gravel, grading, shoring up shoulders, and maintaining drainage systems, such as culverts, swales, and screens.

F: FIRE-RESISTANT PLANTS

Plant fire-resistant ground covers if the shoulders of the roads are landscaped. These plants are resource conserving, less flammable, and able to recover quickly from damage, whether from fire or trampling. Irrigate just enough to maintain adequate leaf-moisture content during the fire season. Importantly, make sure that all ground covers, whether planted or not, are kept down to 6 inches by midsummer.

G: PROTECT POWER LINES

Prune weak and spindly vegetation from around power lines. Typically, the electricity distributor is responsible for maintaining its transmission lines. Report problems without hesitation; wildfires started from transmission lines are common. Furthermore, it is far harder to fight a fire without power; streetlights do not work, firefighters cannot see into structures, and water pressure might drop if power lines are not protected.

H: PRUNE TREES

Prune trees so that limbs do not reach across a road, providing a fuel pathway for a fire. However, some neighborhoods encourage overarching trees because of the fantastic cooling effect. If this is the case in your neighborhood, then:

- Use Zone 1 or 2 trees. See Chapter 9 ("The Zone Theory") for more information.

- Constantly remove dead, dying, and diseased branches and stems.

- Maintain adequate leaf moisture. Nearly all the plants recommended for fire protection are more effective with irrigation.

- Rake up leaf litter.

- Mow ground covers within 5 feet around a tree's dripline to no more than 6 inches high, which should help stop a ground fire from climbing into the tree.

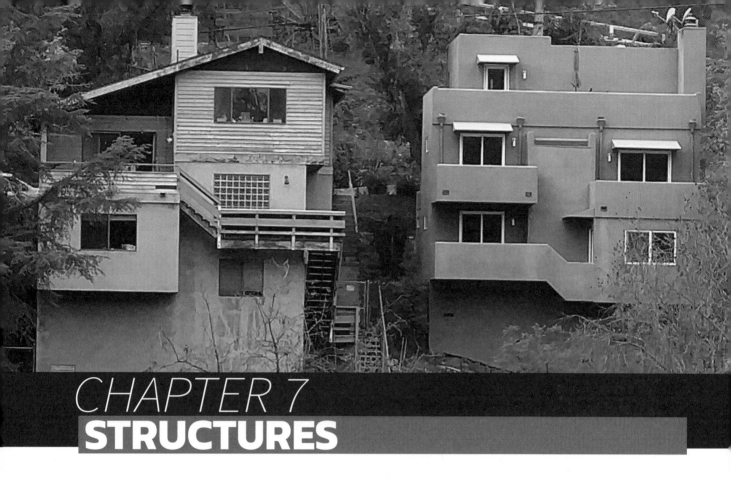

CHAPTER 7
STRUCTURES

We will never be able to keep fire out of natural and native landscapes—and we may never want to—but we can absolutely stop it from consuming our homes. A majority of the structures destroyed during a wildfire were ignited by a firebrand, which is a flying ember driven ahead of the fire. What may look benign during the cool months can become an explosive liability during fire weather. A rusted vent screen, a small pile of clothes left out for donation, or peeling paint can catch a firebrand and fuel it. When firebrands rain on a structure for days, even the smallest lapse in design or maintenance can have a devastating impact. This chapter includes the most important design features of a protected structure. Maintenance for structures is covered in Chapter 16 ("Maintenance Priorities").

Top: These two houses sit in stark contrast. The one on the right is well maintained and has double-paned windows and nonflammable siding and overhangs. The one on the left is just the opposite. **Above:** Even with a metal roof, this structure is at risk of fire because of poor maintenance.

IS YOUR HOME SAFE?

You are more likely to lose your home to a firebrand than to direct flame contact. A structure that can survive a firebrand assault is constructed of fire-resistant materials. Using the chart below, identify the attributes that best describe your home or building.

ATTRIBUTES	RATING	DETAILS
Wood-shingle roof	Lethal	Best is clay, concrete, or metal. Asphalt is combustible.
Wood-shingle siding	Lethal	Even fire-resistant types become kindling with age.
Deck or other parts of house overhanging a slope	Lethal	Firebrands and heat become trapped.
Roof littered with leaves and branches	Dangerous	These create entry points for fire.
Branches overhanging a chimney by 10 ft. or less	Dangerous	Overhanging vegetation will lead a fire to a structure.
Clutter and debris around structure	Dangerous	These restrict movement and give firebrands opportunities to ignite.
Flammable plants next to the structure	Dangerous	They can catch firebrands and ignite.
30 years or older	Bad	Older homes lack fire-resistant features that new homes must have, such as fire-resistant siding.
Class A roof (such as clay, concrete, or metal), fire-resistant siding, and no flammable items or plants within 5 feet	Safe	Your home has a good chance of survival.

DESIGN CHECKLIST

Fire raining from the sky—that's firebrands. These wind-propelled embers can shower a property and community for days, if not weeks, during a conflagration. Designing and maintaining a home that can withstand this wind-driven assault is paramount to protection. The letters in the illustration on page 36 correspond to the letters below. Follow the listed recommendations to give your structure the best chance of surviving an onslaught of firebrands and heat.

A: ROOF Firebrands will assault a roof, which is by far the most important feature of a fire-hardened home. A good roof will be fire resistant, consisting of only Class A materials, such as metal, clay, or concrete tile. Replace wood shingles. The roof should be only slightly slanted, not highly pitched, and should follow the direction of the property's slope.

Outlets for heat and sparks must be protected. Install spark arresters above chimneys and stovepipes. Screens should be made from corrosion-resistant, noncombustible wire mesh with gaps no larger than ½ inch and no smaller than ⅜ inch.

B: ROOF ACCESS Plan for easy access to the roof. Whether the design is simply a convenient and stable platform to raise a ladder, or a series of steps, creating access to the roof is important not only for ease of structure maintenance but also for firefighting and providing a lookout.

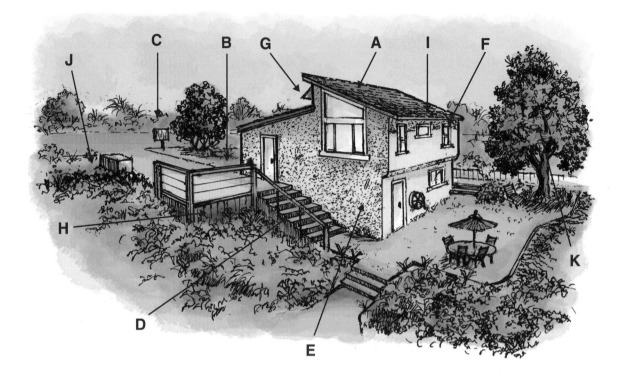

C: **SITE ADDRESS** The property's address must be visible from 50 feet away and during times of reduced visibility. An effective sign will have at least a 70% contrast between the background and the characters. The characters should be at least 6 inches tall, although 8 inches is better (ensuring visibility from 60 feet away in clear conditions). It is always wise to make signs from non-flammable materials.

D: **ENTRANCES AND EXITS** Swift and safe travel is crucial. Stable paths that lead from the parking area to all sides of the structure are vital. The walkway should be at least 4 feet wide, with a 2% cross slope to shed water, and the surface should be able to accommodate caster wheels. Concrete, decking, crushed rock, and compacted earth work with wheels. Lighting is common on critical paths. Refer to Chapter 11 ("Small Properties") for more detail.

E: **SIDING** Noncombustible siding, such as stucco and stone, is the second-most important characteristic in saving a structure. If the siding is wood, then it must have a 1-hour fire-resistance rating and should be constructed with no cracks or deep seams. Wood shingles are not recommended.

Above: An effective house number has numbers at least 6 inches tall, with high contrast between the background and the characters. **Top:** The letters in this illustration correspond to the design checklist for structures described in this chapter.

Although the paneling on this house looks like wood, it is made from fiber cement and is fire and heat resistant.
Photographed by Adam Rowe

Surrounded by eucalyptus and its litter, this deck will definitely ignite during a wildfire. The unskirted deck will catch all the heat, sparks, and wind that the fire creates. A skirt is a barrier, such as gypsum board and metal sheeting, that runs from the bottom of the deck to the ground.

F: WINDOWS All windows should be made from tempered glass and be either double- or thermal-paned. Furthermore, and if possible, keep the windows facing the high fire danger small, so that they will be unable to transmit the heat of the fire into the structure. Replace fabric curtains with louvers, shutters, or fire curtains.

G: AIR VENTS Ventilation holes in the structure must be protected from firebrands. Air vents should be designed smaller in fire country and should be screened with mesh that is noncombustible, corrosion resistant, and no greater than ⅛ inch (although 1/16 inch may be recommended in extra-high fire risk areas).

H: DECKS Decks should be made from brick, tile, or concrete. If wood is used, the planks should be joined using tongue-and-groove construction, leaving no gaps between boards, and the wood should have a 1-hour fire-resistance rating. Decks must be designed with a slope of no less than 1.5% to avoid standing water.

The underpinning of decks and structure overhangs should be enclosed with a nonflammable skirt, such as concrete blocks, gypsum boards, or metal siding. A less effective but more economical skirt is enclosing the overhang with ⅛-inch wire mesh. If a skirt is not used,

then certified ignition-resistant lumber should be used for the supporting members, and the undersides should be coated with a nonflammable material, such as plaster or stucco. Items that are even remotely ignitable are never, ever stored under unprotected overhangs.

I: EAVES Eaves should be small or coated with nonflammable material, such as stucco, or a fire-resistant soffit should be installed. See below for more information.

PROTECTING YOUR EAVES AND HOUSE

Big eaves help cool a structure and create a more hospitable living environment. But they are dangerous in fire country because they trap firebrands and heat. Below are two strategies for reducing the risk.

1. If the eave is open and the rafters exposed, coat with nonflammable finishes, such as plaster, stucco, or fire- and heat-resistant paint.

2. Enclose the eave with a horizontal soffit. The material must have a 1-hour fire-resistance rating, such as fire-resistant-treated lumber, fiber-cement board, or plywood coated in stucco.

Exaggerated for sun protection, the eaves on this structure have been enclosed with a fire-resistant soffit. Notably, the accessories, such as fasciae and gutters, are also fire resistant.

J: STORAGE Store compost, firewood, recyclables, and other flammable items 30 feet away and uphill of the house. If these items are stored in a container, it must be constructed of nonflammable materials, such as sheet metal, cement board, or wood with a 1-hour fire-resistance rating.

K: TREE LIMBS Keep limbs and large shrubs 15 feet from the structure and 10 feet above the roof.

A welcoming driveway is a key feature of a fire-protected property.

This structure has many winning characteristics. Double-paned windows, fire-resistant siding, and an entryway soffit with fire-resistant coating provide excellent protection against fire-brands and heat.

ATTRACTING EMERGENCY PERSONNEL

During a conflagration in which multiple homes are aflame, emergency personnel have to decide, from within a truck and sometimes in a matter of seconds, which ones are the best use of their equipment, time, and manpower. These professionals will not risk their lives for a structure that provides poor protection and limited opportunities to safely defend it.

More specifically, firefighters are looking for an area where they can drive in and turn around; an area that can handle the distribution of equipment; escape routes if people have to flee on foot; and enough vegetation clearance around the house to ensure a degree of safety. Below are the specifics that will help your house be more attractive to firefighters.

- A large driveway that allows fire trucks to easily get to a structure and then turn around.

- A house where flammable vegetation has been removed 30 feet from all sides of the structure.

This large gravel driveway has plenty of room for fire trucks to maneuver and set up equipment.

- Visually and physically accessible and safe routes around the structure.

- A roof that is nonflammable and easily accessible.

- Skirting on decks or other features that overhang a slope.

- Open spaces where equipment and hoses can be laid out, such a large driveways, patios, and grassy areas.

- Flammable vegetation and clutter cleared from around outbuildings, stored vehicles, and liquefied petroleum gas (LPG) tanks.

- Clear sight lines to resources that would help a professional battle a wildfire, such as stored water (such as a cistern, pond, pool, or spa), hoses, ladders, shovels, and water pumps.

CHAPTER 8
DRIVEWAYS

The driveway is fundamental to protection—it is typically where firefighters stage a defense and is their first impression as they are deciding which homes are the best use of their limited resources.

Trained professionals are methodical in their approach to risk. Firefighters are looking for a clear route to the structure and the means to turn around; they look for clearance around the structure and low density of plants; and they look for escape routes and clear lines of communication. Your driveway should provide a view to all these lifesaving attributes.

DESIGN CHECKLIST

Firefighters are under orders not to risk their lives for homes and properties that are too flammable and unsafe. If the driveway does not look accommodating and safe, they will drive on, looking for a property they

can safely and successfully defend. Refer to the illustration on the opposite page, and follow the corresponding recommendations below.

A: VEGETATION MANAGEMENT Flammable vegetation is removed 5 feet from either side of the driveway.

B: MARKERS If the driveway is narrow and winding, install road-guide markers to help lead people to the structure at night and in times of poor visibility.

C: BRANCHES Tree branches are pruned 15 feet above the driveway.

D: TURNAROUND ABILITY Firefighters will drive down a driveway only if they think they can quickly drive out.

E: ADDRESS The driveway provides a clean line of sight to the structure's address.

Above: These homeowners have built a driveway that will invite firefighters. It can accommodate a fire engine, there is room to scatter equipment, and it allows the truck to back out and flee if needed. Photographed by Adam Rowe

IS YOUR DRIVEWAY SAFE?

ATTRIBUTES	RATING	DETAILS
House is inaccessible from driveway; must walk more than 30 ft. to structure.	Lethal	Having to hike equipment and hoses to a structure increases personal risk.
Dead and dry vegetation lines the driveway.	Dangerous	Unmaintained vegetation can create a fire trap.
Narrow driveway is squeezed by vegetation.	Dangerous	Emergency personnel may lack room to maneuver.
Long, winding driveway has no lights or markers.	Bad	Visibility is terrible during fires.
House and amenities are visible from the street.	Safe	Make firefighters feel safe when driving to your home.

What do firefighters see when they pull up to your driveway?

CHAPTER 9
THE ZONE THEORY

In the middle of a murky landscape stands a lone house. Its walls are a grayish, sticky black, and the ground cover of periwinkle and iris is singed and curled but still green. All surrounding shrubs are ash. The horizon is torn by jet-black, leafless trees. Chimneys and large piles of soot are seen in the distance, the only remains of the neighbors' houses.

The scene described above accompanies almost every fire. In the midst of a charred landscape sits a single home, somehow protected from the fire that consumed all others. This chapter emphasizes the reasons why some houses are able to survive. It is a model from which all landscapes should be designed.

Firescaping's Zone Theory differs from the standard model by addressing the elements that create a beautiful and functional landscape as well as a fire-protected property. Planting for a sense of privacy or holding a hill can unintentionally create a lot of fuel. A good landscape design will not only help defend a home against the threat of fire, but will serve the unique goals of the individuals who care for it as well.

The Zone Theory is perfectly suited for large properties. People who manage small lots, properties on steep slopes, and houses nestled under a grove of trees may find the model cumbersome. Chapter 10 covers slopes; Chapter 11 covers small properties; and Chapter 12 covers ridgetop and understory properties.

Above: The principles of the Zone Theory can help ensure your house survives a wildfire. **Top:** A beautiful fire-protected landscape

IS YOUR LANDSCAPE SAFE?

From a structure to 30 feet out, identify the attributes that best describe your landscape.

ATTRIBUTES	RATING	DETAILS
PLANTS		
Landscape is composed of flammable trees.	Lethal	These plants will catch and then sustain a fire for a long period of time.
Landscape is composed of flammable shrubs and grasses.	Dangerous	These are flash fuels and quickly propel a fire.
Landscape is composed of fire-retardant and fire-resistant plants.	Safe	These plants can catch firebrands without producing significant flames.
Vegetation is dry and brittle and breaks when bent.	Lethal	These plants are kindling waiting for a spark.
Vegetation is dry and withered but still supple.	Dangerous	These plants are reluctant to burst into flames but eventually will.
Vegetation is healthy and supple.	Safe	The landscape catches sparks, produces flames, sustains a fire, and then helps propel it.
SITE'S ASPECT		
Southwest-facing	Lethal	The hottest and driest landscape.
Northwest- or southeast-facing	Bad	These landscapes do not get the sun all day but still dry out.
Northeast-facing	Safe	These landscapes stay cooler and more moist.

A firescaped garden is not just created once but is maintained over its lifetime. Please, read the maintenance chapters (Chapters 16–18) carefully!

ZONE 1: THE GARDEN ZONE/ DEFENSIBLE SPACE

Distance: Extends 30 feet from all sides of a house or structure.

Primary goal: The garden zone/defensible space is the most important zone in this model. Without igniting, this zone must be able to withstand firebrands and intense heat, between 900°F and 1,300°F. Everybody and anybody should be able to move unencumbered and swiftly through the garden zone. Firefighters will battle a blaze within these first 30 feet.

Secondary goals: The garden zone has to maintain high recreational, functional, and/or economic value to remain useful to its occupants. The ideals of beauty and privacy play a large role in determining plant selection. Fences, hedges, sheds, compost areas, and stored items, such as firewood, are common in this zone and add a lot of fuel.

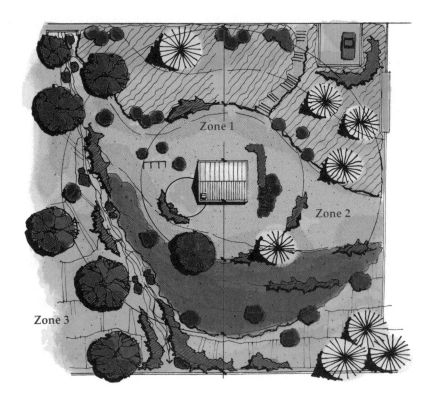

RECOMMENDATIONS

PLANT SELECTION Plants in the garden zone must wilt and sizzle, but not ignite, when exposed to flames and heat. This means that plants in this zone will likely be broad-leaved, supple, and moist. This group is considered fire retardant. Chapter 13 ("Plant Selection and Fire Protection") has Zone 1 plant lists for lawn alternatives, festive perennials, and accent trees.

CARE AND MAINTENANCE The garden zone will consume a disproportionate amount of a landscape's budget. And rightly so—lives are at stake within this zone. The garden zone also consumes the most water, resources, and time. The most fire-retardant plants will require irrigation and attention, more so in arid environments. Food crops, lush understory plantings, and tropical plantings are some examples of high-maintenance plants that survive firebrands and intense heat.

ACCESS AND ESCAPE The garden zone is where firefighters will fight a fire, so wide, stable pathways must surround the entire structure. There should be a place to stage equipment and people, and clear sight lines to escape routes and the surrounding landscape. Everyone should be able to move through this zone with ease, never worrying about ducking, tripping, or getting entangled. On large lots, it is essential to have and maintain two ways off the property. Refer to Chapter 14 ("Landscape Features") for more on paths.

Above: These three properties have designed and maintained an effective Zone 1. Not only will the landscapes help catch and extinguish firebrands, but they are also beautiful and inviting.
Top: An overview of the Zone Theory

GARDEN FEATURES The garden zone may contain a lot of ignitable features: fences, furniture, play structures, shade structures, and storage sheds are common. Naturally, using noncombustible materials, such as metal, is the surest strategy. But there are other strategies too. Refer to Chapter 14 ("Landscape Features") for more detail.

Wrought iron is fire resistant, long-lasting, and sometimes even inviting.

SOURCES OF IGNITION Many places in the garden zone are likely to produce sparks and flames. Barbecues, fire pits, and work areas need to be designed to handle the occasional spark: flammable vegetation must be cleared around them; Zone 1 plants used; and dead, dying, and diseased vegetation constantly removed.

MAINTENANCE Maintenance is the fulcrum of fire protection. Fire must not be allowed in the garden zone,

and the role of maintenance cannot be stressed enough. Refer to the maintenance chapters (Chapters 16–18) for priorities, techniques, and timing of maintenance tasks.

RVS AND TRAILERS

RVs and trailers can be a huge liability during a wildfire: once they ignite, they are incredibly difficult to extinguish. They catch firebrands with canvas contraptions, leafy debris underneath, and openings in paneling and compartments, and they propel a fire with rubber, thin paneling, and stored fuel.

RVs and trailers can be protected:

- Remove awnings and other firebrand-catching appendages.

- Blow or sweep debris from underneath the vehicle.

- Remove flammable vegetation at least 10 feet around the vehicle.

- Install curtains that can deflect heat on all windows.

ZONE 2: THE GREENBELT/ FUEL BREAK

Distance: 31–70 feet from a protected structure. Houses on slopes need to add 10 feet to this zone for every 10% increase in slope. For example, the greenbelt would extend to 120 feet on a property that has a 50% slope.

Primary goal: The greenbelt should stop a ground fire. Select low-growing, hearty, and water-thrifty plants. These plants are the most fire resistant. The effects of droughts, freezes, and occupant neglect should have the least impact in this zone.

Secondary goals: Within view of a house, privacy, aesthetics, and wind protection play important roles in plant selection and placement. These goals add a lot

In Zone 2 of this property, quick-to-ignite flash fuels have been mowed, deadwood has been removed, and islands of view-blocking vegetation have been maintained for privacy.

of fuel to this zone over time. On sloping properties, controlling erosion is one of the most important roles of this zone.

RECOMMENDATIONS

DESIGN A greenbelt might be extensively planted and irrigated, or it might not. It might be large swaths of ground-hugging cotoneaster or natural vegetation mowed to 6 inches. Regardless of the approach, this zone needs to be mostly drought tolerant. The greenbelt must maintain its fire resistance despite irrigation cutbacks, extended system failure, and/or occupant neglect. A majority of the plants in the greenbelt are no higher than 18 inches.

PLANT SELECTION The goals here are low fuels and fire resistance. These plants may produce a small flame, but it quickly goes out. They actively resist the effects of fire. Furthermore, Zone 2 plants should be aggressive enough to outcompete weeds. Chapter 13 ("Plant Selection and Fire Protection") has Zone 2 plant lists for flowering shrubs, hedge plants, and shade trees.

ESCAPE ROUTES Properties that can accommodate the full girth of Zone 2 are fairly large and need at least two ways off the property. The pathways (escape routes) that lead away from the driveway must be readily and visually accessible. One of the first tasks of emergency responders is to identify and communicate escape routes to the crew.

FUEL TANKS Gas tanks should never be closer to a home than 50 feet, which puts them in the greenbelt. Maintain 5 feet of defensible space, such as gravel, mowed vegetation, or Zone 1 plants, around the tank. Importantly, the gas tank area cannot be used as storage, which is, unfortunately, fairly common.

FEATURES Fences, hedges, outbuildings, screens, and water tanks are common in the greenbelt. All these

The area around this fuel tank has been properly cleared of flammable vegetation.

features add fuel and combustibility. Refer to the next chapter ("Landscape Features") for recommendations on overcoming these risks.

ESTABLISHMENT Establishing a planted greenbelt can take up to three years. A planted barrier to both fire and weeds will require time to spread and take hold. Ensuring establishment might entail exhausting the

These property owners are smart and fire-wise. They used a combination of fire-resistant plants, with the most water conserving at the top and the most water demanding at the bottom. The plants are *Myoporum* 'Pacificum,' periwinkle (*Vinca major*), and turf.

soil of stored weed seeds, installing an irrigation system, extensive planting or seeding, creating barriers to migrating seeds, and an annual cleanup.

MAINTENANCE Removing dead, damaged, and diseased vegetation is the best use of maintenance time in the greenbelt, although some other tasks are nearly as important. Refer to the maintenance chapters (Chapter 16–18) for priorities, methods, and timing of tasks.

ZONE 3: THE TRANSITION ZONE

Distance: Starting at 71 feet from a structure—farther on slopes—this zone extends 50 feet out, to 120 feet on flat ground. On smaller lots, the transition zone may only be a row of barrier shrubs.

Primary goal: Dramatically slow a fire.

Secondary goals: The transition zone acts as a buffer between two different types of landscapes: the domestic and the natural. As such, this zone has many functions to perform. Controlling weeds, managing stormwater, reducing erosion, and improving biological diversity sometimes outweigh aesthetics. Plant selection reflects these other goals.

RECOMMENDATIONS

MANAGEMENT Work in this zone mostly involves managing existing vegetation as opposed to establishing a new type of landscape. To help slow a fire, keep trees and large shrubs isolated by two times their mature height, keep wild grasses mowed to 6 inches, and remove vines and shrubs from around and under trees.

PLANT SELECTION If this zone needs planting, it is typically for a specific purpose. Controlling erosion and ecological restoration are two of the goals for planting. Plants selected in the transition area are low-growing and broad-leaved, can survive in native soils, and have the ability to be weaned off supplemental water once established. Many of these plants are native and fire-evolved, meaning that they will not only survive a fire but also quickly resprout after one.

WEED CONTROL The transition zone can help protect the greenbelt from unwanted, flammable weeds. Conversely, it can protect the natural landscape from aggressive exotics. A row of durable barrier shrubs will help stop weed seeds from migrating in either direction.

EROSION CONTROL A properly maintained transition zone is constantly being cleaned and cleared of excess fuel, which can increase the chances of topsoil loss. Both wind and water have greater leverage in landscapes with less cover. If you are managing slopes in fire country, refer to Chapters 10 ("Slopes"), 19 ("First Aid for Fire-Scarred Landscapes"), and 20 (Holding Your Hill: Long-Term Strategies").

MAINTENANCE As in all zones, removing dead, diseased, and damaged vegetation is the most important use of maintenance time. Creating and maintaining access throughout this zone is the second best use of time. Please refer to the maintenance chapters (Chapters 16–18) for priorities, methods, and timing of maintenance tasks for the transition zone.

ZONE 4: THE NATIVE OR NATURAL ZONE/OPEN SPACE

Distance: 121 feet from a protected structure and outward on flat ground, farther out on slopes.

Primary goal: To reduce the severity of a fire.

Secondary goals: To ensure that the natural landscape does not pose an unnecessary risk to the individuals living around it. To maintain the health of the landscape's fauna and flora.

RECOMMENDATIONS

MANAGEMENT The natural/native zone is rarely planted, and simply managing the existing plants and fuels is enough. In the wild areas, there are three approaches to managing excess fuels: mechanical removal, grazing, and prescribed burns. Refer to Chapter 21 ("Community Obligations") and Chapter 22 ("Managing a Community's Three Landscapes") for the specifics of managing wild landscapes.

A good Zone 3

CHAPTER 10
SLOPES

Wildfires on slopes burn hotter, run faster, and produce higher flames than fires on flat ground. For every 10% increase in slope, the length of flame will double, meaning that if a shrubby ground fire produces 6-foot flames, it will lengthen to 24 feet on a 20% slope—more than enough to jump up and into houses and trees.

IS YOUR SLOPE SAFE?

You are more likely to lose your home to a firebrand than to direct flame contact. A structure that can survive a firebrand assault is composed of fire-resistant materials.

SLOPE	RATING	DETAILS
30% or more	Lethal	A 4-ft. flame will grow to 16 ft. or higher on these slopes.
11%–29%	Dangerous	Flame length is still doubled on these slopes.
5%–10%	Bad	Flame length is longer here than on flat ground.
Flat–4%	Safe	The shortest flames are found on flat ground.

Above: With wood siding, unskirted decks, and large overhangs surrounded by unmaintained slopes, these homes have little chance of surviving.

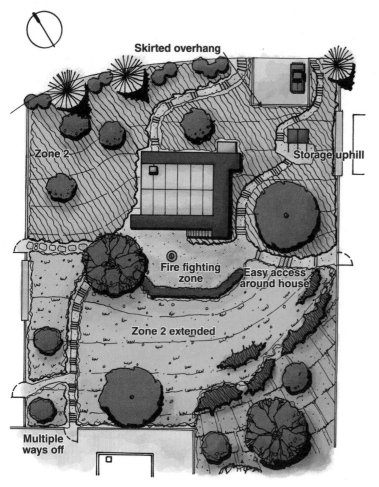

Skirted overhang

Zone 2

Storage uphill

Fire fighting zone

Easy access around house

Zone 2 extended

Multiple ways off

The elements of a successful hillside garden: Paths run throughout the property. A combination of low-fuel fences provide privacy. The compost and firewood storage are placed uphill of the house. And the slope below the house is maintained with aggressive low-growing, ground-hugging Zone 2 plants.

DESIGN CHECKLIST

Homes on sloped properties are particularly prone to damage during a wildfire because of those long flame lengths and the rapidly rising heat. Refer to the illustration at left and follow the listed recommendations.

EXTENDED GREENBELT To reduce flame lengths on slopes, extend the fuel break in proportion to the percent of incline. For every 10% increase in slope, add 10 feet to Zone 2. For example, if your house is on a 15% slope, then the number of feet added to the greenbelt is 15, and the fuel break will extend 85 feet instead of 70.

NOTHING IGNITABLE Anything that could remotely ignite during a firestorm should be removed immediately from around a structure. The heat that fires produce on slopes is intense and can ignite plants and houses 100 feet away. Keep as many of the site's flammable features, such as stored firewood and compost piles, uphill of the structure. Continued on page 52

AMOUNT OF GREENBELT REQUIRED

The table below provides recommendations that might be a part of your local fire code. It sets a standard for the amount of defensible space required according to the type of vegetation and steepness of the slope.

LANDSCAPE TYPE	GREENBELT REQUIRED		
	0–20% SLOPE	21–40% SLOPE	41%+ SLOPE
Grasses, herbs, scattered shrubs	30 ft.	100 ft.	100 ft.
Shrubs	100 ft.	200 ft.	200 ft.
Trees with little or no understory plants	30 ft.	100 ft.	100 ft.

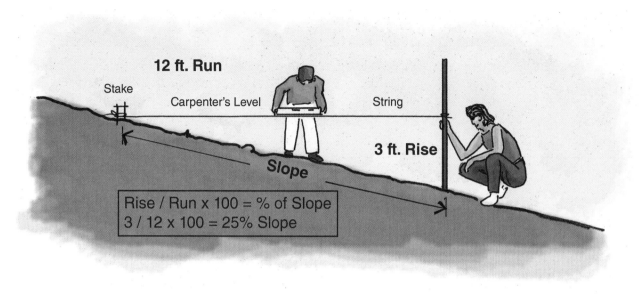

12 ft. Run

Stake

Carpenter's Level

String

3 ft. Rise

Slope

Rise / Run x 100 = % of Slope
3 / 12 x 100 = 25% Slope

Calculating the percent of incline for a slope is relatively easy and takes less than 10 minutes.

MEASURING SLOPE

Calculating percent of incline is easy and requires only a stake, a roll of string, a level, and a board at least 4 feet long. Stake the end of the string to the top of the hill, tie the other end around the board, hold the board vertically, and then walk downhill. Stop when the string is taunt and level, as shown. Measure the string from the stake to the board; this is the run of the slope. The rise of the slope is the distance between the ground and where the string attaches to the board. The percent of a slope is the rise divided by the run, then rounded to the second number and multiplied by 100.

The degree of a slope is different from the percentage. Below is an illustration with the approximate equivalencies for ratio (of rise to run, in feet), percentage, and degree. An engineer's calculator can convert a slope's percentage to its degree.

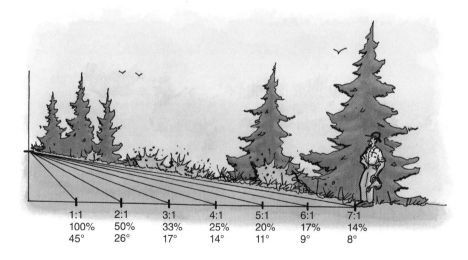

1:1	2:1	3:1	4:1	5:1	6:1	7:1
100%	50%	33%	25%	20%	17%	14%
45°	26°	17°	14°	11°	9°	8°

The illustration above will help you visualize the relationship among a slope's percent of incline, ratio, and degree.

PROPER CANOPY SPACING The distance between the canopies of trees will influence a fire's rate of spread and intensity. Canopy fires are the hardest type of fire to battle. They produce intense heat, send exploding firebrands into the air, and are difficult to reach. Use the guidelines below to design a wooded landscape that will help slow a wildfire.

30 Feet

20 Feet

10 Feet

40% and Beyond

21% – 40%

0 – 20%

Proper spacing between trees is critical on slopes. Both flame length and wind velocity are greater on slopes.

Terracing is simply building a small wall that reduces the length and/or incline of a slope. Many types of material can be used for terracing, and this illustration highlights a few, including stacked blocks, staked boards and logs, soil berms, and riprap.

TERRACING Breaking up a slope's length breaks up a wildfire's flame length—the shorter a slope, the smaller the flame. Terracing also slows a fire's rate of spread. Terraces are small walls that run perpendicular to a slope. They are generally made from nonflammable materials, such as stacked rock, but can also be made from oversized lumber. Terracing can make maintenance easier and reduce long-term costs. However, it demands special maintenance; refer to Chapter 17 ("Maintaining Zones 1 and 2") for specifics.

EROSION CONTROL Every design and maintenance decision you make must reflect a commitment to keep the slope in place. Erosion not only endangers your property and your neighbor's, but it also degrades local bodies of water and stormwater-management systems. Aggressive ground covers that crawl and root along the top of the soil are the best at reducing topsoil loss. Deep-rooted shrubs are good at holding soils together, pulling water from saturated soils, and buffering a slope from wind and rain, but they are not as good as scrambling ground covers at preventing topsoil loss. See Chapter 20 ("Holding Your Hill: Long-Term Strategies") for more detail.

PATHS The more paths a property has, the better. Getting to, through, and off a landscape is as important for emergencies as it is for maintenance, both of which greatly influence a structure's chances of survival. Creating three ways off a landscape is preferred for large hillside properties; two ways is essential.

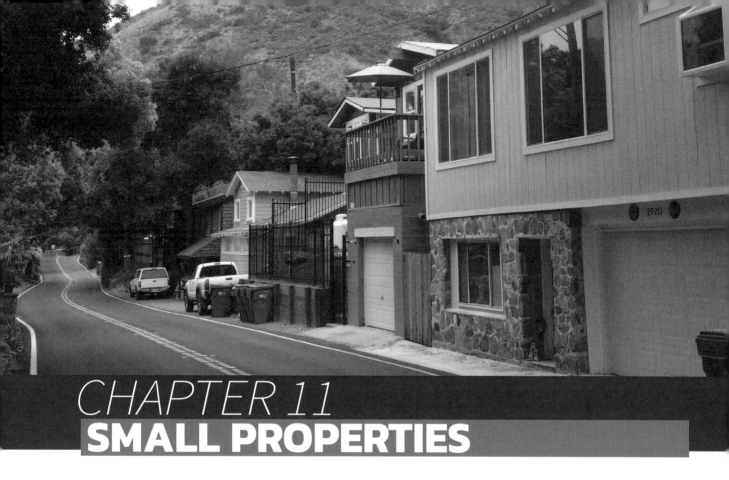

CHAPTER 11
SMALL PROPERTIES

Many of the nation's most destructive wildfires have roared through communities made up of small lots. One house catches fire, and the rest fall like dominoes. Reaching temperatures that can exceed 2,200°F, the radiant heat from a burning structure is enough to ignite anything within 30 feet—and homes on small lots may be no more than 20 feet from each other.

But it's not just the closeness of the structures that makes small properties dangerous; they also have a tendency to accumulate an incredible amount of fuel. Fences, shade structures, dense vegetation, storage sheds, and flammable clutter can all be found within 10 feet of a structure on small lots.

Above: Aged and densely planted vegetation adds unnecessary risk to this small wooded lot. Not only is the property a firebrand trap, but emergency access is greatly hampered as well. **Top:** With a two-lane road, fire resistant materials, off-street parking, great community awareness, and constant maintenance, this neighborhood has survived several wildfires.

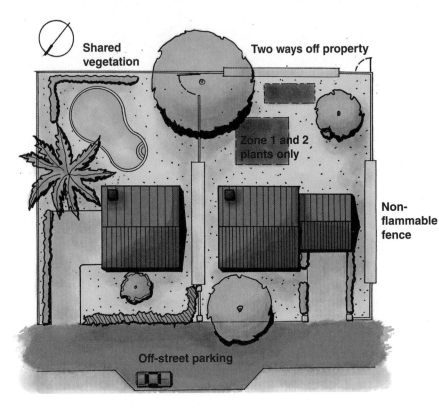

Shared vegetation

Two ways off property

Zone 1 and 2 plants only

Non-flammable fence

Off-street parking

The illustration above shows many of the elements needed for fire protection on small sites. Fire-resistant roofs, off-street parking, proper plants, cinderblock fences, shared vegetation, and access between homes are the ingredients for survival.

DESIGN CHECKLIST

Whether the threat comes in the form of firebrands, intense heat, or direct flame contact, homes on small lots have to defend against a variety of fires. Use the design ideas below to create a property and home that stands a better chance against the assault.

ROOF Installing a fire-retardant roof is possibly the most important factor in protecting a house on a small lot. Firebrands will strike the property long before heat or fire breaches the property lines.

OFF-STREET PARKING Gridlock is common in high-density neighborhoods any time of day, but more so during wildfires, as firefighters are scrambling to get in while residents are scrambling to get out. Off-street parking and pullouts will speed traffic flow. Pullouts should be created even if it means sacrificing a part of your property.

ESCAPE ROUTES Small lots and dense neighborhoods need to have as many escape routes as possible. If the roads are gridlocked, escape by foot is the only other option. Talk with your neighbors and negotiate a gate that can be opened from both sides.

FENCES Privacy fences add an incredible amount of fuel to any property, but this is compounded on small lots. Frequently planted on both sides with dense vegetation and only 5–30 feet from a structure, grape stake fences create a runway for fire. Refer to the next chapter ("Landscape Features") for effective design ideas for fences.

PLANT SELECTION Zone 1 plants are preferred on small lots; they are the most fire retardant. Zone 2 plants can be used, but they can produce flames, and big flames if poorly maintained.

SHARED VEGETATION Not every property needs a tree. Often homeowners can simply let a neighbor's tree grow over and onto their property. Sharing the benefits and maintenance costs of a large tree will create a tree that is healthy, strong, and functional.

POOLS AND SPAS Any type of clean water can be used to help battle a wildfire. Design your pool or spa so that you or firefighters have easy access to the water and drain outlets. Refer to Chapter 15 ("Emergency Water Systems") for design specifics.

CHAPTER 12
RIDGETOP AND UNDERSTORY PROPERTIES

The Zone Theory has an impeccable record of success. However, properties within a high fire hazard will be widely diverse, and not all benefit equally from its recommendations. Better suited for large properties, the Zone Theory is difficult to apply on ridgetop properties and homes nestled under a grove of trees. These situations need a more tailored approach.

RIDGETOP DESIGN CHECKLIST

Properties along the top of a slope are probably the most dangerous. Wildfires can come from any direction. The extremes of heat and cold, wind and rain have their greatest impact on ridgetops. The growing conditions are often so tough that only the most drought tolerant, cold-hardy and flammable plants are likely to survive.

The people living on ridgetops must also be tough. In an emergency they may be asked to play a pivotal role in battling a blaze. If the local fire agency has designated your ridgetop as a place to fight a fire, then they will be strict and diligent in enforcing fire codes.

INDEPENDENCE People living on ridgetops must be able to protect themselves during a wildfire. It is not uncommon for ridgetops to be cut off from community resources during an emergency. People living on ridgetops could lose power and water, and firefighters may not venture up because of the danger. Properties on ridgetops should have a generator, stored water, water pumps, many escape routes, and reliable communication links.

SLOPES All of the characteristics used to protect a house on a slope are also employed on ridgetops, but on all sides. The elements of a fire-protected slope are an extended greenbelt, no ignitable materials, proper distance between trees, terracing, and ground-hugging plants.

Above: This canyon will produce convection-induced winds and extended flame lengths when afire. These condo owners must be vigilant.

The owners of this ridgetop home have taken many steps to defend their home and attract firefighters. An irrigated pasture surrounds the house, and there are no fuel ladders (shrubs) that would lead a ground fire into the pines, which have been well maintained. There is plenty of room for vehicles and equipment, and the vegetation is cleared on either side of the road.

UNDERSTORY DESIGN CHECKLIST

Living under a canopy of trees is beautiful. Noises are muted, the scents are intoxicating, and the vegetation flourishes. However, understory landscapes are dangerous, even with high moisture. Although less ignitable than many other types of landscapes, once a canopy fire gets going, it is exceptionally difficult to extinguish.

A TURNAROUND Fighting a fire from below it is both risky and scary. Firefighters will be reluctant to drive down a driveway if they cannot quickly turn around and escape. A turnaround provides not only the means for escape but also a place to stage a defense.

CAMPGROUND-LIKE FEATURES An effective design idea for properties under a grove of trees is to mimic a campground. To accommodate the campsites, parking, roads, and amenities, trees have to be thinned into distinct islands. These islands create privacy, intimacy, and distinct memories. Moreover, busy campgrounds do not have a lot of wood on the ground, as it has been gathered for campfires.

MAINTAINED IGNITION AREAS Many places are likely to produce sparks and become the source of a fire. Design barbecues, fire pits, and work areas to withstand the occasional spark. Clear flammable vegetation around these areas; install spark arresters on chimneys and small engines; and remove limbs to 10 feet above barbecues and chimneys.

NONSKID SURFACES Whether from leaf fall, algae, or moss, pathways become slippery under a canopy of trees. All surfaces should have a 2% cross slope to shed water. Concrete should be finished with a rough surface, such as brushing. And decking should have gaps to allow for air circulation.

PROPER TREE CARE Maintaining the health of the grove is essential. These trees will either catch firebrands and protect you or ignite and endanger you. The basic rules for tree care are: Ensure proper spacing, avoid changing the grade or trenching within a tree's dripline; irrigate if necessary; and prune with proper technique and timing. Lastly, never hesitate to remove aging trees and plant new ones.

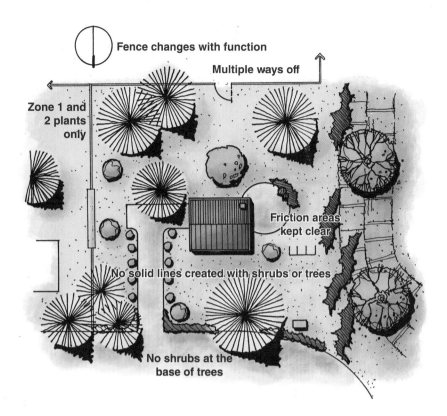

Fence changes with function

Multiple ways off

Zone 1 and 2 plants only

Friction areas kept clear

No solid lines created with shrubs or trees

No shrubs at the base of trees

Above: This illustration highlights some of the characteristics of a fire-protected understory landscape. Overhanging branches have been removed from above the patio and work area. There are no shrubs at the base of the tree trunks. And the grove has been thinned to create structurally independent and strong trees. **Below:** This understory property has many favorable features. An open campground look has been maintained. Zone 1 has been expanded. And importantly, there are no fuel ladders that would lead a ground fire into the trees.

CHAPTER 13
PLANT SELECTION AND FIRE PROTECTION

Vegetation will either lead a fire to a structure or stop it. The plants surrounding a house are one of the most important factors in its chances of survival.

This section is divided into three chapters: Zone 1 plants, Zone 2 plants, and flammable plants to avoid. It focuses on the basics: lawn alternatives, colorful perennials, hedge plants, flowering shrubs, accent trees, and shade trees.

Picking plants for a firescaped garden is tough because at one point or another every plant will burst into flames. All the plants recommended in this section can catch fire, but they are less likely to than others.

For more information about fire-resistant plants, consult online Firewise plant guides, state extension education literature, and regional recommendations from wholesale and retail nurseries.

Above: Even drought-tolerant plants may need an occasional deep watering to maintain adequate moisture. **Top:** The prostrate manzanita pictured above is highly fire resistant. It is also good at suppressing weeds and recovering from foot traffic.

ARE YOUR PLANTS SAFE?

The plants in a landscape must protect not only a structure and its occupants but the neighborhood as well. A poorly designed and maintained landscape increases the risks to all. Identify the attributes that best describe your landscape below.

ATTRIBUTES	RATING	DETAILS
A landscape with a lot of dead or dying vegetation	Lethal	This represents kindling.
A poorly maintained landscape with many close-growing trees and shrubs	Lethal	Not only will this ignite from a firebrand, but it will also produce an incredible amount of heat when inflamed.
A landscape composed of dense shrubs	Dangerous	Flame lengths can reach 20 ft. with dense shrubs.
A grassy landscape intermixed with perennials and subshrubs	Bad	These produce low but fast-moving fires.
Trees and shrubs isolated by 2 times their height	Safe	Fires lack the density of fuels to produce intense heat.
A landscape cleared of dead and dying vegetation	Safe	This landscape will protect the occupants and firefighters.
Dry and brittle vegetation that breaks when bent	Lethal	This is kindling ready to combust.
Dry and withered but still supple vegetation	Dangerous	These plants are reluctant to burst into flames but eventually will.
Healthy and supple vegetation	Safe	These plants are capable of resisting fires.

CHARACTERISTICS OF LESS FLAMMABLE PLANTS

Whether or not a plant will catch fire, keep a fire going, or propel a fire is determined by its characteristics. Getting to know the traits of less flammable plants is more important than remembering plants lists.

A less flammable plant will have:

- Deciduous rather than evergreen leaves.

- Large and broad rather than needle- and bladelike leaves.

- Leaves that are moist and easily bent instead of stiff and leatherlike.

- Thick instead of fine or thin leaves.

- A low amount of litter.

- Sap that looks more like water, as opposed to thick, gummy, or resinous sap.

- Leaves and stems without a heavy fragrance, as opposed to strong aromatic qualities.

- Leaves that are silver or gray.

- Leaves without hair (cilia).

THE TWO TYPES OF RECOMMENDED PLANTS

Plants recommended for a firescaped garden can be divided into two groups: fire retardant and fire resistant.

FIRE-RETARDANT PLANTS

The plants used in Zone 1 are considered fire retardant. They will sizzle and wilt when exposed to flames and heat but are reluctant to produce a flame. If properly maintained, these plants can catch and extinguish firebrands. The trade-off for this protection is irrigation. Most of these plants need supplemental water to maintain adequate moisture and health. Succulents are a notable exception.

Coral bells (*Heuchera* spp.) thrive on the cooler sides of a structure and, if well maintained, can endure intense heat and firebrands without igniting.

FIRE-RESISTANT PLANTS

Fire-resistant plants repel fire. Their leaves and twiggy growth will produce a flame when exposed to fire and heat, but the flame quickly dies. Thick bark and dense wood protect the plant from fully igniting. Many of these plants survive direct flame contact, some resprouting within a month after a wildfire. Using plants that resist fire and rapidly resprout is vital to reducing risk of erosion following a fire. Although fire-resistant plants are drought tolerant, most would benefit from an occasional deep watering.

THE PROBLEM WITH PLANT LISTS

Every plant recommended in this chapter can catch fire. The ability of any plant to retard or resist a fire depends on its condition. Any plant that is old, water starved, infested by pests, or improperly cared for is more flammable as a consequence. Landscape maintenance, not plant selection, is the fulcrum of fire safety.

Elderberry is incredibly fire resistant when young but becomes a firebrand trap when old. Maintenance is truly the fulcrum of fire protection, not plant selection.

FIRE-RETARDANT PLANTS: ZONE 1

Extending 30 feet from a structure, the garden zone must be able to withstand an onslaught of firebrands and intense heat. Below are five plant lists that meet many of the most pressing needs within Zone 1: growing food, lawn alternatives, festive perennials, hedges, and accent trees.

GROWING FOOD

Food crops are fantastically fire retardant and fire resistant. They have all the right characteristics: they have high moisture and big, supple leaves and are generally well maintained. Whether annual, perennial, subshrub, shrub, vine, or tree, food crops offer fire protection, personal health, and maybe even some environmental benefits.

ANNUALS These are some of the most fire retardant because they are 70%–90% water. Crops include beans, beets, chard, corn, lettuce, melons, peas, and zucchini.

BIENNIALS This group of plants generally needs two growing seasons to go from seed to flower. Crops include artichokes, beets, carrots, cauliflower, celery, chard, collard greens, leeks, onions, parsley, parsnips, and turnips.

PERENNIALS Perennials produce fleshy growth and live three to six years. Crops include asparagus, cilantro, mint, potatoes, strawberries, taro, and tomatoes.

SUBSHRUBS This group produces fleshy growth from woody or semiwoody crowns. Crops include basil, lavender, oregano, and sage (cooking).

SHRUBS Plants with woody crowns and stems and no taller than 25 feet are shrubs. Crops include blueberries, cranberries, elderberries, gooseberries, pomegranates (dwarf), raspberries, and salal.

VINES Options include blackberries, boysenberries, grapes, kiwifruit, and passion fruit.

TREES Apple, apricot, avocado, banana, cherry, citrus (all), crabapple, fig, nectarine, mango, mulberry, pecan, pear, persimmon, plum, and pomegranate.

LAWN ALTERNATIVES

Lawns provide two huge benefits. First, they are fire resistant and stubbornly difficult to ignite. And second, they are a fantastic surface from which to fight a fire. Unfortunately, turf also consumes large quantities of water, and municipalities have been reluctant to recommend it. Below is a list of plants that use less water than turf, can tolerate some foot traffic, and, if properly cared for, will not ignite when attacked by firebrands and heat.

The plants listed below are mostly fleshy, spreading perennials that root along their stems. This group can recover from trampling and damage.

Gazania (clumping and trailing), Santa Barbara daisy (*Erigeron karvinskianus*), and verbena have replaced a lawn on this small lot.

LAWN ALTERNATIVES

COMMON NAME	BOTANICAL NAME	USDA ZONES	HEIGHT	LEVEL OF SELF-REPAIR (good, OK, poor)	BLOOMS (spring, summer, fall, winter)
Ajuga, carpet bugle	*Ajuga* spp.	3–9	2 in.–1 ft.	Good in the right spot, OK everywhere else	Spring
Alumroot, coral bells	*Heuchera* spp.	4–9	9 in.–2 ft.	OK	Spring/summer
Bellflower	*Campanula* spp.	3–9	6 in.–4 ft.	Good–poor, depending on variety	Summer/fall
Bird's foot trefoil	*Lotus corniculatus*	4–9	6 in.–2 ft.	Good–OK	Spring/summer
Chamomile	*Chamaemelum nobile*	4–9	3–8 in.	Good in the right spot	Summer
Cinquefoil	*Potentilla* spp.	4–9	3–6 in.	Good	Spring
Cranesbill	*Geranium* spp.	1–10	6 in.–1.5 ft.	OK	Summer
Creeping phlox, moss phlox	*Phlox subulata*	3–9	3–6 in.	OK–poor	Spring
Creeping red fescue	*Festuca rubra*	3–10	3–9 in.	Good	N/A
Dead nettle	*Lamium* spp.	3–9	6 in.–1 ft.	OK	Spring/summer
Dwarf plumbago	*Ceratostigma plumbaginoides*	5–9	6 in.–1 ft.	OK	Summer
English, Hahn's, and smaller-leafed ivies	*Hedera helix, H.* 'Hahn's,' *H.* 'Needlepoint'	4–9	6 in.–2 ft.	Good	N/A
Fleabane	*Erigeron* spp.	2–11	9 in.–2 ft.	Good–OK	Spring
Gazania	*Gazania* spp.	8–11	6 in.–1 ft.	Good–OK	Spring/summer
Hedge nettle, betony	*Stachys* spp.	4–9	6 in.–1.5 ft.	Good	Summer
Indian mock strawberry	*Duchesnea indica*	5–9	3–6 in.	Good–OK	Summer
Irish and Scotch moss	*Sagina subulata*	4–8	1–3 in.	Good	Spring
Lippia	*Phyla nodiflora*	8–11	3–6 in.	Good	Spring
Mexican evening primrose	*Oenothera speciosa*	4–9	6 in.–2 ft.	Good	Spring/summer
Pachysandra	*Pachysandra* spp.	4–9	6 in.–1 ft.	Good	Spring/summer
Periwinkle	*Vinca* spp.	4–11	4–9 in.	Good	Spring
Rockcress	*Arabis* spp.	2–9	4 in.–2.5 ft.	Poor	Spring
Rupture wort	*Herniaria glabra*	5–10	1–3 in.	Good	N/A
Strawberry and white clover	*Trifolium* spp.	3–10	3–6 in.	Good	Spring
Tickseed	*Coreopsis auriculata* 'Nana'	4–9	6 in.–1 ft.	OK–poor	Spring
Thyme	*Thyme* spp.	5–9	3 in.–1.25 ft.	Good–OK	Spring/summer
Viola	*Viola odorata*	4–8	4–9 in.	Good	Spring
Wild aster	*Aster* spp.	4–9	9 in.–4 ft.	Good–poor	Summer/fall
Wild bergamot, beebalm	*Monarda fistulosa*	3–9	2 ft.–4 ft.	OK–poor	Summer
Wild strawberry, sand strawberry	*Fragaria* spp.	3–10	3 in.–1 ft.	Good	Spring
Yarrow	*Achillea* spp.	3–9	6 in.–2.5 ft.	Good	Summer
Zoysia	*Zoysia* spp.	7–11	3–6 in.	Good–OK	N/A

SUN (full, partial, shade)	WATER NEEDS (dry, moderate, moist)	NOTES
Needs shade in warm climates	Moderate	Prefers rich soil
Prefers shade in warm climates	Dry–moderate	
Needs shade in hot climates	Moderate–moist	Tough in good soil
	Moderate	Mow if looking rangy. Can be invasive.
Can tolerate some shade	Moderate	Not the true herb chamomile
Prefers some shade in hot climates	Moderate	
Most species prefer a little shade.	Dry–moderate	Most species prefer rich soil.
	Moderate	Does best in rich soil
Needs some shade	Dry–moderate	Does not grow well in poor soil
	Moderate	With good soil and regular water, it will be aggressive.
	Dry–moderate	Can help hold hills
	Moderate	Do not use *H. canariensis* (Algerian ivy) because of its flammable thatch and invasive nature.
	Dry–moderate	Cut back if lanky.
	Dry–moderate	Reliable and aggressive in good soil
Deer resistant and drought tolerant in shade	Dry–moderate	
	Moderate	Can be invasive if well watered and fed
Best with a little shade	Moderate	
	Dry–moderate	Tough and deer resistant
	Dry	Tough but can be invasive
	Moderate	Slow grower, but tolerates foot traffic
	Moderate–moist	Can become invasive. Mow if looking tired.
	Dry–moderate	Some varieties can be short-lived.
Prefers filtered shade in hot climates	Moderate	
	Moderate	Able to fix nitrogen and help poor soils; can be invasive
	Moderate	Deer resistant and can naturalize
	Dry–moderate	Mow if looking rangy.
	Moderate–moist	Aggressive in rich, well-draining soil
	Dry–moderate	There's one for every garden.
Looks best with moderate water	Dry–moderate	Tolerates a wide variety of soils
Needs shade in hot climates	Moderate	Mow or cut back if rangy.
Does best with a little shade	Dry–moderate	
	Dry–moderate	Looks like lawn but rarely needs mowing

Terraced, mowed, semi-irrigated, accented with small fruit trees, and bordered with naturalizing bulbs (daffodils, iris, and narcissus), this greenbelt has great access and low fuels. It can help stop a ground fire. Photographed by Adam Rowe

Mexican bush sage

FESTIVE PERENNIALS

Perennials are dynamic and committed to community connections. They evolve soils, and the majority are animal pollinated, supporting bees, butterflies, and many other important pollinators.

Technically, a perennial is any herbaceous (nonwoody) dicot that lives longer than two years. Grasses are monocots, and shrubs and trees are woody dicots. This section also includes some plants that are considered subshrubs—the plants like mallow that sit between perennials and shrubs.

The plants listed below have beautiful blooms, low fuel, and relatively high moisture content.

SALVIAS

Salvias can be beneficial or detrimental; some varieties merely wilt in fire-driven heat, while others readily explode. They are worth special mention because all are interesting and beautiful, and almost every garden can grow one or two.

Mexican bush sage (*Salvia leucantha*) is fire resistant because of its supple leaves and stems, low-fuel interior, and ability to quickly resprout after fire or injury.

FESTIVE PERENNIALS

COMMON NAME	BOTANICAL NAME	USDA ZONES	HEIGHT	BLOOM TIME (spring, summer, fall, winter)	WATER NEEDS (dry, moderate, moist)
Bear's breech	*Acanthus mollis*	7–10	3–5 ft.	Early summer	Moderate
Bergenia	*Bergenia* spp.	3–9	9 in.–1.5 ft.	Spring	Moderate
Black-eyed Susan	*Rudbeckia* spp.	3–9	2–3 ft.	Summer/fall	Dry–moderate
Blanket flower	*Gaillardia* spp.	3–10	1–3 ft.	Summer/fall	Moderate
Bluebells	*Hyacinthoides* spp.	4–9	6 in.–1.5 ft.	Spring	Moderate–moist
Columbine	*Aquilegia* spp.	3–9	1–2 ft.	Spring	Dry–moderate
Coreopsis	*Coreopsis* spp.	4–9	6 in.–2.5 ft.	Spring/summer	Moderate
Coneflower	*Echinacea purpurea*	3–8	2–5 ft.	Summer	Dry–moderate
Daylily	*Hemerocallis* spp.	3–9	1.5–3 ft.	Summer	Dry–moderate
Flax	*Linum* spp.	3–9	6 in.–2 ft.	Summer	Dry–moderate
Foxglove	*Digitalis* spp.	4–8	2–5 ft.	Spring	Moderate
Garden penstemon	*Penstemon* spp.	3–10	1–3.5 ft.	Summer/fall	Dry–moderate
Gaura	*Gaura lindheimeri*	5–9	1.5–3 ft.	Summer	Dry–moderate
Gayfeather	*Liatris* spp.	3–9	2–4 ft.	Summer	Dry–moderate
Hooker's evening primrose	*Oenothera* spp.	4–9	1–6 ft.	Summer	Dry–moderate
Hosta	*Hosta* spp.	3–9	1–2 ft.	Summer	Moderate–moist
Indian paintbrush	*Castilleja* spp.	3–10	1–3 ft.	Spring/summer	Dry
Lupine	*Lupinus* spp.	3–10	1–3 ft.	Spring/summer	Dry–moist, depending on species
Mallow	*Malva* spp.	3–9	1–3.5 ft.	Summer	Dry–moderate
Maximilian sunflower	*Helianthus maximiliani*	4–8	Up to 10 ft.	Summer	Moderate
Milkweed	*Asclepias tuberosa*	3–9	1–2.5 ft.	Summer	Dry–moderate
Prairie coneflower, Mexican hat	*Ratibida* spp.	3–9	1–3 ft.	Summer	Dry–moderate
Red hot poker	*Kniphofia uvaria*	5–9	2.5–4 ft.	Spring	Moderate
Poppy	*Papaver* spp.	2–10	1–4 ft.	Spring/summer	Moderate–moist
Spurge, Mediterranean spurge, gopher plant	*Euphorbia characias, E. myrsinites, E. rigida*	6–9	1.5–3 ft.	Spring	Dry–moderate
Wallflower	*Erysimum* spp.	5–9	6 in.–2 ft.	Spring/summer; can be short-lived, so let the flowers go to seed.	Dry–moderate

White sage

As white sage (*Salvia apiana*) ages, it becomes easier to ignite and harder to extinguish.

A fire-resistant sage will have supple leaves and stems on a woody base. Some of the good sages for fire protection include germander, pineapple, desert, Mexican bush, and Caradonna meadow (*Salvia chamaedryoides, S. dorrii, S. elegans, S. leucantha,* and *S. nemorosa*).

Some of the sages that can catch and hold a flame include white, Cleveland, purple, black, and wand (*S. apiana, S. clevelandii, S. leucophylla, S. mellifera,* and *S. vaseyi*).

HEDGES

The wrong type of hedge will lead a wildfire to a structure. A well-designed and maintained hedge will do just the opposite. The plants listed below will be reluctant to ignite, have large leaves, are somewhat slow growing (avoiding a dense, twiggy interior), and do not create excessive litter. Refer to Chapter 14 ("Landscape Features") and Chapter 16 ("Maintenance Priorities") for more detail.

Important: All hedges will have to be replaced at some point. Do not let a fire force you to do it.

For about half its life, *Nerium oleander* is fantastic at repelling firebrands and heat. But like all plants, it becomes more flammable with age.

HEDGES

COMMON NAME	BOTANICAL NAME	USDA ZONES	HEIGHT	BLOOMS (spring, summer, fall, winter)	SUN (full, partial, shade)	WATER NEEDS (dry, moderate, moist)	FOLIAGE (deciduous, evergreen)
Buckthorn, coffee-berry, redberry	*Rhamnus* spp.	2–8	5–7 ft.	Spring	Full–partial	Dry–moderate	Deciduous and evergreen varieties
Camellia	*Camellia* spp.	7–9	5–12 ft.	Fall/winter/spring	Partial	Moderate–moist	Evergreen
Carolina allspice, spice bush, sweetshrub	*Calycanthus* spp.	4–9	6–13 ft.	Spring/summer	Full–partial	Moderate	Deciduous
Currant, gooseberry	*Ribes* spp.	2–10	3–9 ft.	Spring	Full, partial–shade	Moderate–dry	Evergreen and deciduous varieties
Elaeagnus, oleaster	*Elaeagnus ebbingei*	7–9	6–10 ft.	Fall	Full	Moderate	Evergreen
Evergreen euonymus	*Euonymus japonicus*	6–9	6–12 ft.	N/A	Full–partial	Moderate	Evergreen
Flowering quince	*Chaenomeles* spp.	4–8	6–12 ft.	Spring	Full–partial	Moderate	Deciduous
Japanese aralia	*Fatsia japonica*	8–10	8–15 ft.	On and off all year	Full–partial	Moderate	Evergreen
Japanese aucuba	*Aucuba japonica*	7–9	6–10 ft.	Spring	Full–partial	Moderate	Evergreen
Japanese mock orange, tobira	*Pittosporum tobira*	9–10	10–20 ft.	Spring	Full–partial	Moderate–dry	Evergreen
Jojoba	*Simmondsia chinensis*	9–10	3–10 ft.	Spring	Full	Dry	Evergreen
Laurel	*Prunus laurocerasus, P. lusitanica*	4–9	6–30 ft.	Spring	Full–partial	Moderate	Evergreen (other deciduous); most species are good screens.
Mock orange	*Philadelphus* spp.	4–10	4–6 ft.	Spring	Full–partial	Moderate–dry	Deciduous
Osmanthus, sweet olive, fragrant olive, devilwood	*Osmanthus* spp.	6–11	8–25 ft.	Spring	Full–partial	Moderate	Evergreen
Photinia	*Photinia × fraseri*	7–9	8–10 ft.	Spring	Full	Moderate–dry	Evergreen
Privet	*Ligustrum* spp.	6–10	4–12 ft.	Spring	Full–partial	Moderate–dry	Evergreen
Sumac	*Rhus* spp.	3–9	6–30 ft.	Spring/summer	Full–partial	Dry–moderate	Evergreen and deciduous varieties
Viburnum	*Viburnum* spp.	2–8	3–20 ft.	Spring	Full–partial	Moderate–moist	Evergreen and deciduous varieties

The crape myrtle is an ideal accent tree in fire country. It is deciduous, is relatively small, has broad and supple leaves, and does not produce vast amounts of debris.

ACCENT TREES

Accent trees are used to engage a viewer, create spaces, and block views. They are typically small and have one or two seasons of interest, such as a flowering in spring and/or having dynamic foliage in fall. With proper maintenance, these trees are capable of protecting a structure by catching and extinguishing firebrands.

ACCENT TREES

COMMON NAME	BOTANICAL NAME	USDA ZONES	HEIGHT	BLOOMS (spring, summer, fall, winter)	WATER NEEDS (dry, moderate, moist)	FOLIAGE (deciduous, evergreen)
Desert willow	*Chilopsis linearis*	7–9	15–20 ft.	Spring/summer	Low–moderate	Deciduous
Dogwood	*Cornus* spp.	4–9	15–30 ft.	Spring	Moderate	Deciduous
Ginkgo, maidenhair tree	*Ginkgo biloba*	3–8	20–80 ft.	Spring	Moderate	Deciduous
Hawthorn, thorn apple	*Crataegus* spp.	3–8	20–35 ft.	Spring	Moderate	Deciduous
Horse chestnut, buckeye	*Aesculus* spp.	3–10	20–75 ft.	Spring	Moderate	Deciduous
Orchid tree	*Bauhinia* spp.	9–11	15–25 ft.	Winter/spring	Moderate	Evergreen
Redbud	*Cercis* spp.	4–8	12–25 ft.	Spring	Moderate–dry	Deciduous
Silk tree/mimosa	*Albizia julibrissin*	6–9	20–40 ft.	Summer	Moderate	Deciduous
Smoke tree	*Cotinus* spp.	4–8	10–30 ft.	Spring	Moderate	Deciduous
Strawberry tree	*Arbutus unedo*	7–10	10–20 ft.	Fall	Moderate–dry	Evergreen
Fruit trees	There is a tree for every zone.					
Chinese pistache	*Pistacia chinensis*	6–9	25–35 ft.	Spring (insignificant)	Moderate–dry	Deciduous
Crape myrtle	*Lagerstroemia* spp.	6–10	15–25 ft.	Summer	Moderate–dry	Deciduous
Michelia	*Michelia* spp.	9–10	25–35 ft.	Winter/spring	Moderate–moist	Evergreen
Ornamental pear	*Pyrus* spp.	5–10	15–50 ft.	Winter/spring	Moderate	Deciduous and evergreen varieties
Silver bell, snowdrop tree	*Halesia* spp.	4–8	15–40 ft.	Spring	Moderate	Deciduous
Sophora, Japanese pagoda tree, mountain laurel, mescal bean	*Sophora* spp.	4–8	10–75 ft.	Summer	Moderate–dry	Deciduous and evergreen varieties
Yellow bells, yellow elder	*Tecoma stans*	8–12	5–18 ft.	Summer/fall	Moderate–dry	Evergreen

FIRE RESISTANT: ZONE 2

Extending 31–70 feet from a structure, and much farther on slopes, the greenbelt stops a ground fire. Plants recommended in Zone 2 are considered the most fire resistant because they can maintain a level of resistance despite drought, infestations, and neglect. Included in this section are lists for succulents and cacti, flowering shrubs, and large shade trees.

SUCCULENTS/CACTI

A succulent is a plant that actively stores water in its stem, leaves, and roots. All cacti are succulents, but not all succulents are cacti. Cacti are distinguished from other succulents by their spines and hairs: cactus spines grow in clumps called areoles; the spines of others succulents do not.

With low fuels and high moisture, succulents are mostly fire retardant. Combine that with their low water use and ease of care, and these plants will not only help protect a structure, but can also provide dramatic statements, energizing colors, and exciting forms.

Their only disadvantage is their limited growing range. As a rule, noncactus succulents do better on the coast, where there is little danger of excessive heat and frost. Cacti do better inland, where there is less danger of moisture and rot. Neither do well with freezing or snow.

Noncactus succulents are used immediately around a structure, and cacti farther out. Not only do noncactus succulents need more water and attention than cacti, but they are also less likely to injure someone. Any plant that is likely to stab or poison a firefighter should be planted 30 feet or more from a structure.

These homeowners have established a hillside garden with succulents. This planting scheme is fire retardant, drought tolerant, and low maintenance. The succulents have also been mostly successful at outcompeting the flammable weeds that have overrun nearby properties.

WATER NEEDS OF SELECT SUCCULENTS

Some succulents do not need irrigation; others will need it year-round. Use this guide to help create your succulent hydrozones.

LITTLE TO NO SUMMER WATER	NO WINTER WATER	MAY NEED YEAR-ROUND WATER
Aeonium	Aloe	Beaucarnea
Agave	Escobaria	Bulbine
Cotyledon	Euphorbia	Calandrinia
Dudleya	Ferocactus	Crassula
Escobaria	Lemaireocereus	Dadyliron
Ferocactus	Opuntia	Echeveria
Haworthia		Epiphyllum
Lemaireocereus		Furcraea
Nolina		Gasteria
Opuntia		Pachyphytum
Senecio		Portulacaria
Yucca		Sedum
		Sempervivum

Succulents such as *Aeonium undulatum,* commonly known as saucer plant, are more fire resistant because of the amount of water they retain in their leaves.

Low-growing sedum can be used as a ground cover.

FLOWERING SHRUBS

Large flowering shrubs define outdoor spaces, block views, and help pull a viewer into a landscape with interesting blooms and structure. The shrubs listed below bloom profusely and are easy to grow, and most have favorable associations with wildlife.

Few shrubs can beat the rose on ease of care and fire resistance.

Clethra

Chaste tree

Hydrangea

FLOWERING SHRUBS

COMMON NAME	BOTANICAL NAME	USDA ZONES	HEIGHT	BLOOMS (spring, summer, fall, winter)	WATER NEEDS (dry, moderate, moist)	FOLIAGE (deciduous, evergreen)
Beautyberry	*Callicarpa* spp.	5–10	3–8 ft.	Spring	Moderate–moist	Deciduous
Bluebeard	*Caryopteris* spp.	5–9	2–8 ft.	Summer/fall	Moderate–dry	Deciduous
Butterfly bush	*Buddleja* spp.	5–9	3–12 ft.	Summer/fall	Moderate	Evergreen and deciduous varieties
Chaste tree	*Vitex* spp.	5–10	1–25 ft.	Summer/spring	Moderate	Deciduous
Clethra	*Clethra* spp.	3–9	3–8 ft.	Summer	Moderate–moist	Deciduous
Coral bean, Cherokee bean	*Erythrina herbacea*	7–10	3–4 ft.	Winter/spring	Dry–moderate	Deciduous
Daphne	*Daphne* spp.	7–9	3–5 ft.	Spring	Moderate–moist	Evergreen–semi-evergreen
Desert honeysuckle	*Anisacanthus* spp.	7–8	3–5 ft.	Summer/fall	Dry–moderate	Deciduous
Elderberry	*Sambucus* spp.	3–10	6–20 ft.	Spring/summer	Moderate–moist	Deciduous
Hydrangea	*Hydrangea* spp.	3–10	3–15 ft.	Summer/fall	Moderate–moist	Deciduous
Lilac	*Syringa* spp.	3–7	4–25 ft.	Spring	Moderate	Deciduous
Red yucca	*Hesperaloe parviflora*	5–11	1–4 ft.	Summer	Dry	Evergreen
Rockrose	*Cistus* spp.	8–11	1.5–5 ft.	Spring/summer/fall	Dry	Evergreen
Rose	*Rosa* spp.	2–11	2–8 ft.	Spring/summer/fall	Moderate	Evergreen and deciduous varieties
Spirea, bridal wreath	*Spiraea* spp.	3–8	2–8 ft.	Spring/summer	Moderate–moist	Deciduous–semi-evergreen
Tree mallow	*Lavatera* spp.	6–10	2–15 ft.	Summer/fall	Moderate–dry	Evergreen
Tropical hibiscus, Confederate rose	*Hibiscus* spp.	7–11	4–15 ft.	Spring/summer/fall	Moderate–dry	Evergreen and deciduous varieties
Yellow bells, yellow elder	*Tecoma stans*	8–12	5–18 ft.	Summer/fall	Moderate–dry	Evergreen

Dusty miller is fire resistant, low maintenance, and a reliable spreader.

GRAY IS GREAT, MOSTLY

Plants with gray leaves are some of the toughest. They survive some of the driest environments by pulling minerals from the soil and reflecting sun. The high mineral content of these plants also makes them fire retardant/resistant. As an added benefit, during the day they make other plants stand out, while at night they can make the entire landscape stand out.

Some of the most fire-resistant gray-leaved plants are listed on the opposite page. However, not all plants with gray leaves provide protection; some are almost incendiary. Refer to the list of flammable plants at the end of this chapter (page 78).

GRAY PLANTS

COMMON NAME	BOTANICAL NAME	USDA ZONES	HEIGHT	BLOOM TIME (spring, summer, fall, winter)	WATER NEEDS (dry, moderate, moist)
GROUND COVERS					
Lamb's ears	*Stachys byzantina*	4–8	6 in.–1.5 ft.	Spring/summer	Dry–moderate
Parrot's beak	*Lotus berthelotii*	8–12	6 in.–1 ft.	Spring/summer	Dry–moderate
Silver sage	*Salvia argentea*	5–9	6 in.–1 ft.	Summer	Dry–moderate
Snow-in-summer	*Cerastium tomentosum*	3–8	6 in.–1 ft.	Spring/summer	Dry–moderate
PERENNIALS					
Artichoke	*Cynara scolymus*	7–11	3–4 ft.	Spring/summer	Moderate
Cooking sage	*Salvia officinalis*	4–10	1–2 ft.	Late spring	Dry–moderate
Dusty miller	*Jacobaea maritima*	3–10	9 in.–1.5 ft.	Spring, summer, fall	Moderate–dry
Maltese cross, crown pink	*Lychnis* spp.	3–10	1–3 ft.	Spring/summer	Dry–moderate
Painted fern	*Athyrium* (many varieties)	3–9	1–3 ft.	N/A	Moderate
SUCCULENTS AND CACTI					
Agave	*Agave franzosinii* 'Grey Ghost,' *A. parryi*, *A. macroacantha*, *A. havardiana*, *A. macroacantha*, *A. parrasana*, *A. potatorum*, *A. tequilana*	7–10	1.5–8 ft.	They are mono-carpic (they die after flowering) but are easily propagated.	Dry–moderate
Echeveria	*Echeveria* spp. (many varieties)	9–11	3 in.–3 ft.	Summer/fall/winter	Dry–moderate
Pig's ear	*Cotyledon orbiculata*	6–10	2–4 ft.	Summer/fall	Dry
Silver coral senecio	*Senecio scaposus*	9–11	9 in.–1.5 ft.	Summer	Dry–moderate
SHRUBS					
Bush germander	*Teucrium fruticans*	8–9	4–8 ft.	Intermittent all year	Dry
Jerusalem sage	*Phlomis fruticosa*	7–10	2–4 ft.	Summer	Moderate
Russian sage	*Perovskia* spp.	4–9	1.5–5 ft.	Summer/fall	Dry–moderate
Texas ranger, silverleaf	*Leucophyllum* spp.	8–11	2–8 ft.	Spring/summer/fall	Dry
Woolly butterfly bush	*Buddleja marrubiifolia*	7–10	4–6 ft.	Spring/summer	Dry–moderate
TREES					
Olive	*Olea europaea*	8–10	15–30 ft.	Summer	Moderate
Pineapple guava	*Feijoa sellowiana*	8–11	15–25 ft.	Spring	Dry–moderate
Silver maple, sugar maple	*Acer saccharinum*	3–8	40–80 ft.	Spring	Moderate
Silver tree	*Leucadendron argenteum*	9–11	25–40 ft.	Inconspicuous	Dry–moderate

LARGE SHADE TREES

Large shade trees are typically placed outside of Zone 1 because they simply possess too much fuel to be any closer to a structure.

The trees listed on the opposite page are recognized as fire resistant, and some are even fire retardant. Furthermore, these trees are low maintenance, are fairly tall (35–70 feet), and provide above average shading.

If well maintained, the red maple (*Acer rubrum*) can withstand firebrands and heat. It also provides great shade and fantastic fall color.

LARGE SHADE TREES

COMMON NAME	BOTANICAL NAME	USDA ZONES	HEIGHT	BLOOMS (spring, summer, fall, winter)	WATER NEEDS (dry, moderate, moist)	FOLIAGE (deciduous, evergreen)
Ash	*Fraxinus* spp.	3–10	40–80 ft.	Spring	Moderate	Deciduous–semi-evergreen
Big-leaf maple	*Acer macrophyllum*	6–10	30–75 ft.	Spring	Moderate	Deciduous
Carob	*Ceratonia siliqua*	9–11	30–40 ft.	Spring	Moderate–dry	Evergreen
Catalpa	*Catalpa* spp.	4–9	25–70 ft.	Spring	Moderate–moist	Deciduous
Chinese elm	*Ulmus parvifolia*	4–9	40–60 ft.	Summer/fall	Dry, moderate–moist	Deciduous
Common hackberry	*Celtis* spp.	2–10	40–80 ft.	Spring	Moderate–moist	Deciduous
Eastern hop hornbeam	*Ostrya virginiana*	3–9	25–40 ft.	Spring	Moderate	Deciduous
European beech	*Fagus* spp.	3–9	50–80 ft.	Spring	Moderate	Deciduous
Ficus	*Ficus* spp.	9–12	25–60 ft.	Winter	Moderate–moist	Evergreen
Kentucky coffee tree	*Gymnocladus dioicus*	3–8	50–80 ft.	Spring	Moderate	Deciduous
Locust	*Robinia* spp.	4–8	40–70 ft.	Spring/summer	Moderate–dry	Deciduous
Magnolia	*Magnolia* spp.	4–9	15–80 ft.	Spring	Moderate	Evergreen and deciduous varieties
Mayten tree	*Maytenus boaria*	9–10	30–50 ft.	Spring	Moderate–moist	Evergreen
Mesquite	*Prosopis* spp	6–10	25–30 ft.	Spring/summer	Dry–moderate	Deciduous–semi-evergreen
Oak	*Quercus* spp.	3–10	30–80 ft.	Spring	Dry, moderate–moist	Evergreen and deciduous varieties
Walnut	*Juglans* spp.	3–10	40–100 ft.	Spring	Moderate	Deciduous

ZONE 3: THE TRANSITION ZONE

Starting 71 feet from a house and extending to 120 feet, and much farther out on slopes, this zone dramatically slows a fire. Transitioning from a domesticated landscape to a natural or native one means that management is more important than plant selection in this zone. Management means encouraging native species, creating adequate distance between shrubs and trees, eradicating invasive plants, and controlling erosion.

If this zone truly transitions, as opposed to being an extension of Zone 1 or 2, then the plants selected should be native. They must be able to survive and reproduce without supplemental irrigation, fertilization, or pest controls. They should also be able to outcompete weeds. Consult your local native plant society, your state extension office, or a grower of native plants for fire-resistant varieties appropriate for your site.

FLAMMABLE PLANTS

The plants listed below create highly ignitable and highly combustible conditions—some will even ignite without flame contact. Ideally, these plants should be removed from Zones 1 and 2 and dramatically thinned in Zone 3.

However, some of the plants listed below have qualities that may be valuable in certain landscapes. Coyote brush (*Baccharis pilularis*) is a good example. In autumn this flammable shrub is one of the few nectar plants in Southern California's coastal scrub communities. There are hundreds of insects that interact with it. One of them, the tachina fly, eats caterpillars from nearby crops. Encouraging coyote brush helps reduce the need for insecticides. Take the time to get to know all the plants on your landscape.

The plants in this median provide little benefit to the residents. They are mostly dead, are highly flammable, and should be removed.

FLAMMABLE PLANTS

BOTANICAL NAME	COMMON NAME
TREES	
Abies spp.	Fir
Acacia spp.	Acacia, wattle
Arecaceae	Palms (if dead fronds not removed and trunk cleaned)
Calocedrus decurrens	Incense cedar
Casuarina spp.	Beefwood
Cedrus spp.	Cedar
Chamaecyparis spp.	False cypress
Cryptomeria japonica	Japanese cryptomeria
Cupressocyparis leylandii	Leyland cypress
Cupressus spp.	Cypress
Eucalyptus spp.	Gum
Larix spp.	Larch

BOTANICAL NAME	COMMON NAME
TREES *(CONTINUED)*	
Laurus nobilis	Sweet bay
Melaleuca linariifolia	Flaxleaf paperbark
Picea spp.	Spruce
Pinus spp.	Pine
Pseudotsuga spp.	Douglas-fir
Sequoia sempervirens	Coast redwood
Taxodium spp.	Bald cypress
Taxus spp.	Yew
Thuja spp.	Arborvitae
Tsuga spp.	Hemlock
Umbellularia californica	California bay, myrtlewood
PERENNIALS AND SHRUBS	
Adenostoma spp.	Chamis, greasewood
Artemisia spp. (many varieties)	Wormwood, sagebrush
Baccharis pilularis	Coyote brush
Brassica campestris, B. nigra	Field and black mustard
Cytisus spp. and *Spartium junceum*	Broom
Dodonaea viscosa	Hopseed bush
Eriogonum spp.	Buckwheat
Haplopappus pinifolius	Pine goldenbush
Juniperus spp.	Juniper
Larix spp.	Larch
Larrea tridentata	Creosote bush
Leptospermum spp.	Tea tree
Platycladus orientalis	Oriental arborvitae
Rosemarinus officinalis	Rosemary
Rubus spp.	Bramble
Salvia apiana, S. clevelandii, S. leucophylla, S. mellifera, S. vaseyi	White, Cleveland, purple, black, wand sages
Tamarix chinensis	Salt cedar
Ulex europaeus	Common gorse
GRASSES	
Hordeum vulgare, Avena sativa, Secale cereale	Annual grasses: barley, oats, and rye
Agropyron repens	Quackgrass
Cortaderia spp.	Pampas grass, jubata grass
Miscanthus sinensis	Eulalia grass
Muhlenbergia rigens	Deer grass
Pennisetum setaceum	Fountain grass

CHAPTER 14
LANDSCAPE FEATURES

A wildfire is not considered bad if it consumes only a few outbuildings or fences. But any landscape feature that was destroyed is bad because the flaming object caught, sustained, and probably propelled the fire. These features brought a wildfire closer to someone's home and life.

Landscape amenities increase ignitable material and hinder movement. Some of the most dangerous are featured in this chapter: paths, fences, shade structures, outbuildings, and hedges. Not included in this chapter are benches, planter boxes, and fuel and water tanks. Fuel tanks are discussed in Chapter 9 ("The Zone Theory"), and water tanks in Chapter 15 ("Emergency Water Systems").

Fire-resistant landscape features will have the following core characteristics:

- Nonflammable materials, such as iron, concrete, or stone, are used.

- If made from wood, then only lumber with a 1-hour fire-resistance rating is used.

- Only Zone 1 or Zone 2 plants (preferably Zone 1) are used around features.

- Flammable vegetation is removed 10 feet from around all features.

- Features are well maintained, which might mean painting the structure, pruning surrounding plants, and removing old plants.

- Replacement is planned, budgeted, and not delayed when the feature is at the end of its lifespan.

Above: This inexpensive barrier to entry will eventually become a visual barrier as the privet grows. This fence is not only effective but will also be fire resistant for many years.

Our flammable footprint can be reduced in many small ways. Keep reading to discover many of them.

GARDEN PATHS

Whether you are fleeing or fighting, rapid travel is essential. Garden paths can become critical components of emergency mobilization. Pathways should be easily identifiable and easily navigated, and everyone should be able to move easily, never worrying about ducking, tripping, or being entangled. The key characteristics of a good path are highlighted below.

WIDTH The path should be at least 4 feet wide and able to accommodate two-way traffic and heavy equipment.

SURFACE The surface should be even, stable, and nonskid (which means no screed concrete).

VEGETATION: Dead and otherwise flammable vegetation must be removed from within 3 feet of both sides of the path. Overhanging branches must never get lower than 10 feet off the ground.

SLOPE The slope of a path should never exceed 5%, which is a 1-foot rise over a 20-foot length. Ramps, which should be made from nonskid concrete, are the exception, and their slope should never exceed 8.3%.

CROSS SLOPE The path should have a 2% cross slope to shed water, which should reduce the chances of puddling water and slippery surfaces. The cross slope should fall upslope, and the runoff managed in a swale. Slanting the cross slope downhill will erode both the path and the slope.

VISIBILITY A minimum of 20 feet of forward visibility should be both designed and maintained.

HANDRAILS Handrails must accompany steps. This benefits not only people who need assistance but also people hauling heavy equipment.

LIGHTING Recommended on critical pathways, such as those that lead from a road to a structure, lighting makes a huge difference in times of limited visibility.

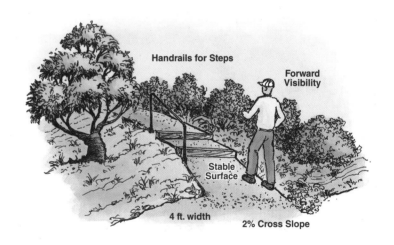

A good garden path

FENCES

Fences can become freeways for fires. They are typically constructed with softwood lumber and lined on both sides with plants that get dense, littered, and twiggy—a perfect environment for firebrands and fires. There are, however, many strategies to reduce the risk.

The first step in designing a low-risk fence is to identify the function(s) the fence must serve. The second step is restricting the flammable material to serving only that function. And the third step is to either restrict the use of plants along the fence or incorporate them into the design. Below are the four primary functions of fences and the best strategies for fire safety.

A practical, low-fuel fence keeps the wood to only the areas needed to screen a view. Wire mesh is used elsewhere. Plants can also be incorporated, as shown, to further increase privacy.

2. Barrier to Entry

This can be the least flammable and cheapest of all fences—its only objective is to keep animals and people out of a space. Neither wood nor plants are needed for this type of barrier.

This is what danger looks like. The old wooden fence and dying cypress create a huge threat to the two wooden houses that sit on either side of it.

THE FOUR FUNCTIONS OF FENCES

The four primary functions of a fence are visual barrier, physical barrier, sound barrier, and aesthetic division. The design solutions for each function are listed below.

1. Visual Barrier

Creating privacy is the top reason for fences. Many people would make them 20 feet tall if they could, but building codes typically prohibit such heights. Hedges are often planted along fences to increase the height of the visual barrier.

DESIGN SOLUTIONS Overcoming the inherent flammability of wood fencing means isolating the risk to only the areas that screen views. Wood panels do not have to run to the ground or along the entire length. Furthermore, the closer the fence is to the people to be screened, the less materials required.

Designing a fence with a solid bottom helps keep weed seeds from being blown onto the property. A solid barrier, however, is not needed farther up. Wire mesh will keep everything else off the property. Plants are added to this design for aesthetics only.

DESIGN SOLUTIONS Chain-link fences and fences made of strong wire mesh stretched between concrete-anchored posts are relatively inexpensive, easy to install, and long-lasting. Below are two examples.

3. Aesthetic Divisions

The only goal here is to make a distinction. Examples include identifying the line between public and private properties; delineating various spaces within a property, such as a driveway or path; or making an aesthetic statement as to what lies beyond, as often seen at the entrances of housing tracts.

DESIGN SOLUTIONS An aesthetic or visual distinction does not require a lot of fuel. Most of the best materials are nonflammable, such as boulders, stacked rock, and pillars. If wood is used, use only oversized lumber with a 1-hour fire-resistance rating, which is fairly common to ranch-style aesthetics.

This trail fence is an aesthetically appealing and relatively inexpensive way to distinguish between public right-of-way and private land.

4. Sound Barrier

This is the most expensive type of fence. The best materials for sound abatement are brick, concrete, decorative blocks, and stucco. Thin slats of wood and plants do a poor job of deflecting noise. Fortunately, not only are the best materials the most fireproof, but they are also long-lived and nearly maintenance-free. Note that the closer a sound barrier is to the sound, the more effective the barrier will be.

PATIENT PLANTING

An overplanted landscape creates continuous lines of plant fuels; it promotes structurally dependent plants; and it can increase the amount of pest damage. Overplanting also increases maintenance costs. When designing your landscape, always plan on a plant's mature size.

These olives, although fire resistant, are planted too close together. They will create a twiggy, dense, and flammable wall when they mature. They grow to 25–30 feet tall and wide, yet they have been planted only 12 feet apart.

SHADE STRUCTURES

Arbors, gazebos, and pergolas add charm and romance to a landscape, but they also add risk. Shading devices are typically placed up against a structure; are made from soft woods; and might have plants growing in, around, and on top of them. Shade structures are prone to ignition.

DESIGN SOLUTIONS

FIRE-RESISTANT WOOD All structures must be constructed with lumber that has at least a 1-hour fire-resistance rating. Although more expensive, steel posts are even better.

PAINT OR STAIN Treating and maintaining a shade structure with paint or stain—preferably fire and heat resistant—not only extends the life of the wood but also fills its fissures, reducing opportunities for firebrands, insects, and fungus to take root.

ENCOURAGE AIR CIRCULATION Materials such as shade cloth, plywood, and fiberglass panels are often installed on top of shade structures to improve shading. Unfortunately, these devices will trap firebrands and heat, increasing chances of ignition. Instead, limit the materials to only where the shading is necessary, and only use nonflammable materials, such as tin and fire-rated plastic sheets. Furthermore, make sure there are gaps between the structure and house.

USE ZONE 1 PLANTS Only the most fire-retardant plants should be used around wooden shade structures. Zone 1 vines include Boston ivy, clematis, jasmine, table grape, and trumpet vine.

PLAN ON REPLACEMENT The life span of a wooden shade structure ranges from 10 to 20 years, depending on the environment and amount of care. The structure will need replacing when the wood starts fracturing or splintering, the joints begin to split, or it shows the signs of extensive termite damage or rot. One of the clearest signs that the structure needs replacement is when it no longer holds paint.

Good air circulation, fire-resistant lumber, and Zone 1 plants increase the safety of shade structures.

OUTBUILDINGS

Garden and tool sheds, well houses, woodsheds, and storage shacks are structures on a landscape that increase its amount of fuel. Like a house, an outbuilding can be designed to be fire resistant.

DESIGN SOLUTIONS

Refer to Chapter 7 ("Structures") for a more in-depth discussion of defensible structures.

ROOF The roof has one of the greatest impacts on a structure's chances of survival. Use Class A roofs only. Exercise extreme caution when contemplating wood-shake roofs with fire-retardant chemicals. Chemical retardants are relatively short-lived and can lose their effectiveness within five years.

PITCH Never design an outbuilding with a highly pitched roof. The steeper a roof, the more firebrands it will catch. A roof should be only slightly slanted, its pitch going in the direction of the slope of the property.

EAVES Overhanging roofs provide many benefits, such as shade and rain protection, but avoid using them on outbuildings. Instead, plan on building thicker walls, ensuring proper insulation, and installing rain gutters to keep water away from the base of the structure.

SIDING Ideally, the material enclosing the structure should be nonflammable, such as metal sheeting, stucco, or rock. If you do use wood, never use wood shakes. Rather, use only wood that can be installed with no gaps or fissures (tongue-and-groove construction fits this requirement), and make sure the wood has a 1-hour fire-resistance rating.

OPENINGS The doors, windows, and vents of an outbuilding should always face uphill—never downhill and in the direction of a likely fire.

WINDOWS Windows are an entry point for heat and fire. To reduce the risk, windows should be small, double-paned, and never facing the area where a wildfire is likely to come from.

OVERHANGS If the structure or any part of it, like decking, overhangs a slope, you must take corrective design measures. Skirt the overhang with nonflammable siding, such as concrete blocks, gypsum boards, or metal siding. A less effective but more economical skirt is enclosing the overhang with ¼-inch wire mesh. If a skirt is not used, then oversized lumber, such as 6-by-6-inch beams and posts, should be used for the supporting members, and the undersides should be coated with a nonflammable material, such as plaster, stucco, or fire- and heat-resistant paint. Never store items that are even remotely ignitable underneath unprotected overhangs.

DEFENSIBLE SPACE Like homes, outbuildings need 30 feet of defensible space around them. Refer to Chapter 9 ("The Zone Theory") for more detail.

With metal sides, the opening facing away from the slope, and plenty of clearance around it, this outbuilding design may survive a wildfire.

HEDGES

Hedges are almost as common as fences; they serve nearly all the same functions. They are also just as flammable, if not more so. A hedge's beauty often masks a flammable interior—one that is impregnable, brittle, and mostly dead. Hedges can easily become a freeway for fires. They quickly get this way when plants are grown too close together and routinely sheared.

DESIGN SOLUTIONS

USE ZONE 1 PLANTS Design your hedge with only the most fire-retardant plants. If the hedge is 30 feet from a structure, Zone 2 plants are acceptable.

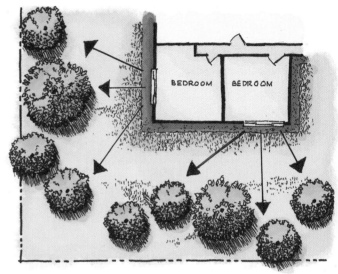

Staggering shrubs helps slow the spread of fire from one to the other.

STAGGER If a property has the space, then there is no need for a continuous line of plants. The hedge can be staggered instead.

ISOLATE Keep your hedge away from other flammable features, such as shade structures, outbuildings, and wood piles.

KEEP CLEAR The landscape around a hedge should either be kept clear of flammable vegetation or be planted with Zone 1 plants.

IRRIGATE No matter how drought tolerant your hedge may be, if its leaf-moisture content drops below 30%, it will ignite. Summer and fall irrigation is necessary for a majority of hedge plants.

MAINTENANCE Refer to Chapter 17 ("Maintaining Zones 1 and 2") for the details of hedge maintenance.

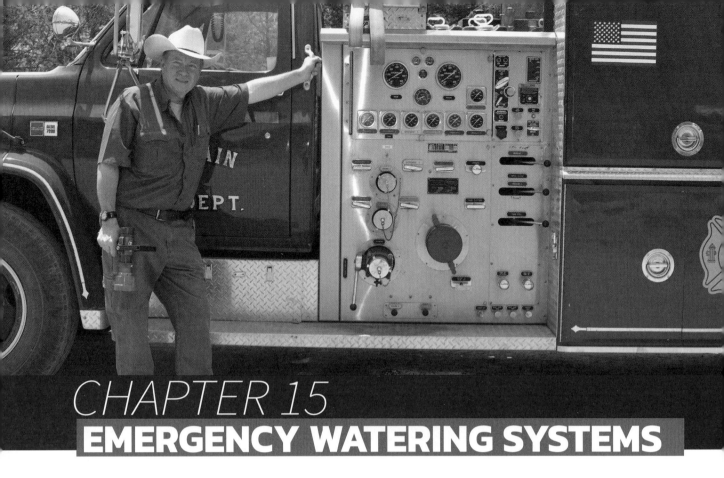

CHAPTER 15
EMERGENCY WATERING SYSTEMS

An emergency watering system has two goals. First, the water is used to raise the ignition tolerance of the house and landscape, increasing the amount of time and heat required to ignite them. And second, it is used to help extinguish incoming firebrands and the small fires they create.

An effective emergency system must be able to compensate for two possible events during a wildfire: power outages and dramatic drops in water pressure. Properties at high elevations and in rural areas are more prone to these two problems, and their emergency water system will have to be independent of the municipal water and power supply.

Above: An emergency watering system is always ready: it has a water source that is naturally filled, it can power and pump itself, and it has hose hookups.
Top: A secondhand fire engine is an emergency water system on wheels—and the cost is often less than an RV. This individual actively defends 130 acres and 1,500 rescued animals with a fire truck he purchased for $25,000.
Courtesy of D.E.L.T.A. Rescue

DESIGNING AN EMERGENCY WATER DELIVERY SYSTEM

An emergency water delivery system should be designed for ease of use. But whether or not a water delivery system will work may never be known until an emergency. Always build a system using the highest-quality materials: brass fittings should be used instead of plastic, and galvanized steel pipe instead of PVC.

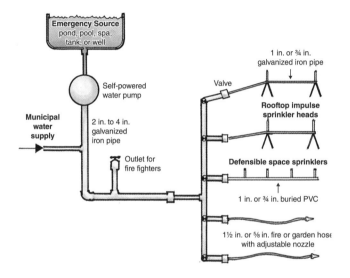

In a good water delivery system, each line can be connected to a municipal water supply or a stored water supply, and there are many water valves so that multiple tasks can be operated collectively or independently.

EMERGENCY WATER SOURCES

Although any amount of stored water can make a difference in combating a blaze, most fire departments recommend at least 1,000 gallons. Any water source over 1,000 gallons should be brought to the fire department's attention. Some fire departments issue blue identification reflectors that help identify emergency sources of water from the road.

Following are the specifics for water sources, access, plumbing, sprinklers, and pumps.

COMMON STORAGE DEVICES

Emergency supplies of water can be stored in a variety of ways. Cisterns, hot tubs, ponds, pools, and water tanks are all excellent storage devices. However, each requires a slightly different approach to make the water readily accessible.

HOT TUBS, POOLS, AND SPAS These common outdoor features are ideal sources of emergency water; they typically have great access, their drainage systems are easy to find and use, and their water is generally free of debris. An emergency water pump and a fire hose are the only accessories needed (see Access and Plumbing Guidelines for Stored Water, page 88, for specifications).

PONDS Making a pond an effective water source requires at least 2 feet of clear water above the debris and murkiness. All water pumps must have a fine-mesh screen over the water intake. You will also need a suction hose no less than 8 feet long. A gas-powered water pump is preferred over electric because of its mobility.

Ponds can be an effective source of emergency water.

WATER TANKS AND CISTERNS Common in high-elevation areas, properties with wells, and water-scarce

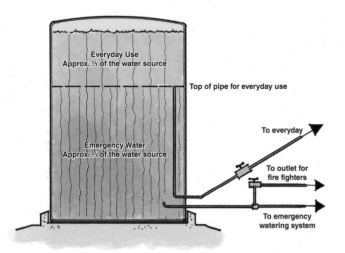

Emergency water is any water in the tank at the time of an emergency. To ensure that there will always be water for an emergency, design the plumbing like the illustration above.

neighborhoods, cisterns and tanks are an excellent source of emergency water (cisterns sit on the ground, and tanks are elevated). These storage devices can be large and are commonly made of steel, redwood, plastic, fiberglass, or concrete. Cisterns require a water pump to effectively move water. Tanks are designed to deliver water via gravity.

ACCESS AND PLUMBING GUIDELINES FOR STORED WATER

Many people in fire country have pools, ponds, or spas, but not all of them can make rapid use of their water because they lack the pumps and large hoses. Below are the access and plumbing guidelines that help anyone make use of stored water in an emergency.

Access

Ideally, a fire truck should be able to drive to within 10 feet of a water source. However, that is rarely practical. An emergency water source should never be farther than 200 feet from the structure it's serving. On hills, the water source should be no more than 50 feet from where a fire truck will park.

No matter how far away the water source, an easy-to-use pathway to it must be created and maintained. The pathway should be at least 4 feet wide. Importantly,

the area immediately around the water source should be cleared of vegetation that would endanger or entangle firefighters.

Plumbing

The drainage pipes of pools, spas, and water tanks need to be readily accessible. They should face the parking/ staging area, be right off a stable pathway, and be easy to spot from a distance.

All drainpipes can be inexpensively modified to make the fittings compatible with a firefighter's hose. Firefighters need a 2½-inch threaded male fitting. A removable reducing bushing can be screwed onto this larger fitting to accommodate a garden hose. Be sure to install a filter on the drainage or intake pipe of all open water sources; clogging is common when pulling water from dirty water sources.

Even 500 gallons of water can make a difference during a wildfire. This tank has many favorable characteristics: A pump is attached to the tank, and it is ready to go (assuming the power does not go out). The drain outlet is easy to get to. And all of this is accessible via a wide and stable path.

SPRINKLER SYSTEM

The goal of an emergency sprinkler system is to soak the landscape, the roof, and/or the sides of a structure during a wildfire. These sprinklers differ from conventional sprinkler systems because they deliver water to the most vulnerable areas only.

The valve, pipe, and sprinkler heads should all be constructed from corrosion-resistant materials, such as brass and galvanized pipe. Valves should be located within sight of the sprinkler heads and should have easy access. Pipes should be buried at least 9 inches deep so they are not crushed by trucks driving over them. And all sprinkler heads should be commercial grade.

Use high-impact sprinkler heads if the area to be covered is large. These heads have a wetting radius of 15–100 feet and can easily irrigate 700–8,000 square feet. High-impact heads that throw 50 feet or more require a 1-inch supply line and 35 pounds per square inch (psi) of water pressure. A head that throws less than 50 feet needs only ¾-inch pipe and 30 psi.

An emergency water-delivery system that is connected to a municipal water supply will have to compensate for the potential loss of water pressure. The sprinkler

This rooftop sprinkler is designed to wet and cool the roof and deck below. This sprinkler will be effective during a wildfire because it is the only head on the line and is made from the highest-quality materials.

system should be able to remain effective with a 55% drop in water pressure. This simply means 55% fewer sprinkler heads for each irrigation line.

WATER PUMPS AND HOSES

With a loss of electricity and/or a big drop in water pressure, a good water pump can be critical in defending a structure. For emergency purposes, there are two types of pumps: electric or gasoline powered.

Electric pumps are generally attached to a structure via an extension cord, and both of these items should be stored together. An electric pump requires an electric generator to keep it running during a power outage.

Gas-powered water pumps are the type used by firefighters. Although gas pumps are more expensive than electric, they are irreplaceable during a power failure or if the water source is a long distance away from the power source (plug). It is important to purchase a pump that can be handled by one person. There are also reliable and portable pumps that run on diesel and propane.

For home protection, look for a pump that delivers water at 100 gallons per minute (gpm) at 50 pounds per square inch (psi) of pressure and has a standard 1½-inch threaded outlet.

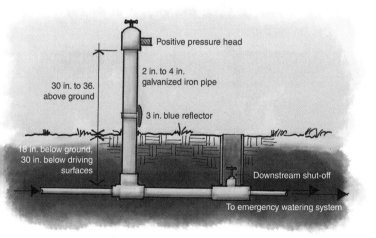

You can create a water-delivery system that is compatible with the needs and equipment of firefighters.

A 250 gpm, 100 psi pump is preferred when moving water long distances. However, even a pump that delivers 50 gpm can help prewet a landscape and extinguish firebrands.

Purchase all water pumps with an 8-foot suction hose, 100 feet of fire hose, and an adjustable fire nozzle. A fire hose is distinguished from other hoses by its fire-resistant jacket.

Pictured above is a formidable defense. A reliable supply of water is plumbed to a pump that is hooked to a 1½-inch-diameter, fire-resistant hose with adjustable nozzle. Courtesy of D.E.L.T.A. Rescue

MAINTENANCE

Proper maintenance is the only way to ensure these systems function when needed—design once, maintain over a lifetime. The elements of a successful maintenance program are below.

TEST THE EMERGENCY WATERING SYSTEM before the start of every fire season.

- Oil and start generators. Always run an engine dry before storing, which helps prevent the gas from gumming up inside the carburetor and cylinders.

- Replace old gasoline with fresh. Aged gasoline has a tendency to turn dark and sour; lose volatility; and gum up filters, lines, and carburetors.

- Test and oil water pumps.

- Impact sprinkler heads may need oiling.

- Turn all valves on and off several times to ensure proper function.

MAINTAIN PATHS that lead to water sources.

- Level the pathways, fixing gullies, rills, and ruts.

- Prune overhanging branches to at least 10 feet above the path.

- Prune any vegetation that has grown onto the path.

- Make sure stairs and handrails are functional and stable.

CLEAN CISTERNS AND WATER TANKS of debris, organic material, and grit every other year, though yearly is best, as accumulated sediment can clog hoses and pumps.

MAINTENANCE

CHAPTER 16
MAINTENANCE PRIORITIES

Every plant, every garden, and every house is flammable. The degree of flammability is directly related to the maintenance the house receives. Poor design, whether architectural or horticultural, does increase the fire risk; however, and more likely than not, it is a lack of maintenance that leads a wildfire to a house.

A property's care must be as ever present as the potential of a wildfire. Maintaining a fire-resistant property will require a list of tasks, priorities for those tasks, and an honest evaluation of the amount of time and money a homeowner can spend on these tasks.

Everything in this chapter, like this book, has been organized to save people first, save a structure second, and protect the community third.

FIRESCAPING'S MAINTENANCE PRIORITIES

- Maintain emergency access.

- Maintain a fire-hardened structure.

- Clean the first 5 feet around a structure.

- Clean and nourish 30 feet around a structure.

- Maintain Zones 2 and 3.

- Help your community.

Above: This house, along with its landscape, is well maintained and fire resistant.

First things first: this chapter has been designed to help you save your family, protect your structure, and aid your community.

1. MAINTAIN EMERGENCY ACCESS

Making sure you and your family can successfully flee is your first and foremost priority. The parts that you manage include the road in front of the property, the driveway, the paths around the house, and the footpaths that lead off your property.

The maintenance of roads is covered in Chapter 6 ("Roads"). And while the design of effective paths is covered in Chapter 14 ("Landscape Features"), their maintenance is covered below.

Fundamental maintenance tasks for paths include:

- Prune overhead vegetation to at least 10 feet above the path.

- Remove vegetation that has grown onto the path.

- Fix or fill uplifted or depressed surfaces.

- Repair, tighten, sand, and paint handrails.

- Replace bulbs in outdoor lighting.

- Maintain nonskid treatments on sloping paths, which often entails washing the surface with a weak solution of bleach and water to remove algae and moss (common in wooded environments).

2. MAINTAIN A FIRE-HARDENED STRUCTURE

The design fundamentals of a protected structure are provided in Chapter 7 ("Structures"). The importance of regular maintenance cannot be understated—houses must be maintained to survive an assault by firebrands. Peeling paint, cracks in surfaces, gaps in flashing, termite-pitted wood, and the underside of eaves littered with spiderwebs all provide an opportunity for a firebrand to inflame a structure. Regular maintenance will drastically improve the chances of your home surviving a conflagration.

Fundamental maintenance tasks include:

- Fixing and filling any fissures and cracks in the siding. If any part of the structure has been treated with paint or stain, reapply it at the first sign of exposure or peeling.

- Cleaning and painting undersides of eaves, and filling gaps.

- Keeping limbs of trees and large shrubs 15 feet from the sides of a structure and 10 feet above its roof.

- Removing leaves and dead material from the roof, from the rain gutters, and immediately around structure.

- Removing ignitable items from immediately around the structure.

- Removing anything remotely ignitable from under the structure and deck. Better yet, skirt the overhanging feature with an ignition-resistant material, such as gypsum board.

- Maintaining easy access to the roof by removing clutter on the ground and overhead obstructions.

3. CLEAN THE FIRST 5 FEET AROUND A STRUCTURE

Many health experts claim that clutter increases stress and anxiety. In fire country, it doesn't just cause stress; it also creates firebrand catchers and home destroyers. It is the Achilles' heel of a fire-resistant home. Clothes, dense plantings, recyclables, stored wood, tools, and toys are just some of the many ignitable items that are regularly stored against a structure.

Fundamental maintenance tasks include:

- Removing clutter. Store items either in the house, in a nonflammable shed next to the house, or 30 feet away from the house.

- Irrigating plants around a house to ensure enough leaf moisture.

- Pruning and removing dead, dying, and diseased vegetation.

- Sweeping up leaves and debris.

- Removing flammable plants. See Chapter 13 ("Plant Selection and Fire Protection") for a list.

4. CLEAN AND NOURISH THE LANDSCAPE 30 FEET AROUND A STRUCTURE

The goal of Zone 1 is to extinguish firebrands and withstand intense heat. Refer to the next chapter (page 99) for the specifics of proper maintenance, which include removal/replanting, managing weeds, maintaining efficient irrigation, and caring for hedges and terraces.

Fundamental maintenance tasks include:

- Pruning and removing all dead, dying, and diseased vegetation.

- Removing flammable plants. See Chapter 13 for a list of flammables.

- Sweeping up leaves and debris.

- Irrigating plants to ensure they have enough leaf moisture.

- Painting, repairing, and replacing landscape features (refer to Chapter 14).

- Removing loose bark and companion plants, such as mistletoe and Spanish moss, from shrubs and trees.

- Cutting all nonirrigated grasses to 6 inches.

- Removing flammable material and combustible ground covers at least 2 feet around the dripline of trees.

- Maintaining proper distances between large islands of vegetation (see page 110).

- Preventing ground covers and vines from scrambling up fences, shade structures, shrubs, trees, and utility poles.

Ivy has consumed this oak tree. Not only will this mass catch a firebrand and ignite, but the aggressive vine is also killing the tree. Vines such as these steal nutrients, restrict a plant's growth to its outermost branches, and can girdle its limbs.

IRRIGATION PRIORITIES

A garden's foundation, the dominant trees and larger shrubs, can either be an effective part of a defensive strategy or an explosive liability. The difference is likely in maintenance. During water shortages, trees and large shrubs should be maintained at the expense of smaller shrubs, ground covers, and perennials, which might have to be sacrificed and removed.

5. MAINTAIN ZONES 2 AND 3

Zone 2 must stop a ground fire, and Zone 3 dramatically slows it. Vegetation management is key in these zones and the outlying areas. Refer to Chapter 18 for details on vegetation management.

Fundamental maintenance tasks include:

- Pruning and removing all dead, dying, and diseased vegetation.

- Removing flammable vegetation and debris around liquefied petroleum gas (LPG) tanks, outbuildings, and wood piles.

- Cutting all nonirrigated grasses to 6 inches.

- Sweeping up leaves and debris.

- Irrigating Zone 2 plants to ensure they have enough leaf moisture.

- Removing flammable material and combustible ground covers at least 2 feet around the dripline of trees.

The letters in this illustration correspond to the list at right.

- Isolating shrubs by two times their height (separate 8-foot shrubs by 16 feet) and trees by three times their driplines (with a 12-foot dripline, the next closest tree should be 36 feet).

- Preventing ground covers and vines from scrambling up fences, shade structures, shrubs, trees, and utility poles.

- Auditing irrigation and stormwater systems, looking specifically for any signs of erosion (rills and gullies), overspray (circular stains), or regular runoff (algae in curbs).

6. HELP YOUR COMMUNITY MANAGE WILDLAND FUELS

A community is made up of far more than individual properties. It also includes public parks, abandoned properties, and road and utility easements, and all these landscapes and structures need care and management. Only a strong commitment to community protection by a large group of people will be able to reduce the risk for an entire area. Refer to Chapters 21 ("Community Obligations") and 22 (Managing a Community's Three Landscapes") for more detail.

PRUNING THE DANGEROUS STUFF

From the simple inconvenience and sometime small scare to downed power lines and extensive property damage, falling branches are a genuine concern for people living in wooded environments. In some cases, the likelihood of fracture is visible before the actual break. Simple inspection is the key. Branches that are likely to split may have some of the following signs. If any of the conditions listed below exist, then remove or support the branch to reduce the risk.

A. Signs of rot, such as shelf fungi (these mean the tree must be removed)

B. Dead, dying, or cracked branches

C. Chafing limbs that cross

D. Branch or limb unions that are tight and V shaped

E. Mistletoe on branches

F. Limbs that are excessively long

CHAPTER 17
MAINTENANCE FOR ZONES 1 AND 2

Zone 1 must be able to endure firebrands and intense heat. Zone 2 must be capable of stopping a wildfire. Because of these lifesaving goals, maintenance in these first two zones is much different than in the outlying areas. These areas are typically planted, irrigated, and regularly used.

In this chapter are guidelines for removal/replanting, managing weeds, maintaining proper plant moisture, caring for hedges, and managing terraces. Guidelines for prioritizing this work are offered in the preceding chapter, "Maintenance Priorities."

FIRST AND FOREMOST: REMOVAL

Nothing is forever; everything has a finite life. For the land manager in fire country, this is a poignant lesson. As plants and landscapes age, they get inherently more

ignitable and combustible. Juvenile landscapes are much less flammable than older landscapes. Juveniles are fleshy, lanky, and low in ignitable material, while older landscapes are brittle, dense, and high in ignitable material.

For these reasons, none of the suggestions or tasks discussed in this chapter is more important than the constant removal of the three Ds: dead, dying, and diseased vegetation. This is the plant material most likely to ignite from a firebrand. Only after Zone 1 has been cleaned of this flammable material should you pursue the other aspects of landscape maintenance. A properly maintained, fire-protected landscape will be in a constant state of renewal.

SIGNS A PLANT NEEDS REPLACING

An old and/or unhealthy plant creates a greater degree of fire risk. These plants are more prone to breakage,

Above: Gravel, small river rock, and decomposed granite are all a part of this well-maintained landscape.

they require more resources and pesticides to sustain, and they may help spread diseases and pests. The characteristics of a plant that needs replacing include:

- Older leaves, stems, and limbs are dead. On trees, 50% or more of the trunk has either dead limbs or no limbs.

- The living foliage is concentrated at the end of the branches instead of throughout the entire branch.

- During summer, the plant drops more leaves than usual.

- The amount of living wood is less than 50% of the entire plant.

- A bud or disease infestation is difficult to control, if possible at all.

- The plant does not recover or is slow to recover from injury.

- The plant shows signs of decay, including mushrooms coming up from its base and roots, or shelf fungi along its trunk.

The false cypress (*Chamaecyparis*) on the far right is too old and highly ignitable. Its interior is crammed with dead and twiggy wood. This plant should be removed.

EVERYTHING HAS A LIFE SPAN

As a landscape nears or passes its expected life span, the risk of fire dramatically rises. Use the generalized table below to budget and plan for the removal of mature plants. As illustrated, a landscape that was planted 50 years ago may require the removal of some, if not most, of the plants.

PLANT GROUP	EXPECTED LIFE SPAN (YEARS)
Large Trees	40–120
Medium Trees	25–80
Large Shrubs	15–30
Small Shrubs	10–20
Vines	8–15 (except asexual vines, like ivy, which root from shoots and roots)
Perennials	3–7
Annuals	1

REPLANTING

Following the tips below will help reduce long-term maintenance costs.

- Do not overplant.

- Allow ample space between new plants, about 1.5 times their mature width.

- Avoid fast-growing plants.

- Always use plants that fit within an irrigation's hydrozone.

- Plant at the proper depth: Mediterranean plants prefer their crown slightly above the soil; temperate plants, even with the soil; and tropical plants, slightly below.

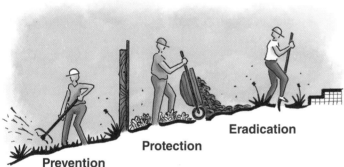

There are three primary parts to managing weeds: prevention, protection, and eradication.

MANAGING WEEDS

This section is built around the three strategies of weed control: prevention, protection and eradication. Prevention stops unwanted plants from getting onto property. Protection stops unwanted plants from either sprouting or spreading. And eradication involves all the techniques and tools used to physically remove weeds.

PREVENTION

Prevention helps stop weeds from traveling onto a property. The techniques employed are controlling the weed seeds on-site and putting up barriers.

CONTROLLING SEEDS ON-SITE It is OK to let weeds grow for a while; in fact, it can even be beneficial. Weeds help break up dense soil, enrich poor soil, and attract pollinators. It is never OK, however, to let unwanted plants go to seed. Letting weeds produce seed guarantees next year's crop will be larger.

If the weeds are high, such as grasses, mow or trim them before they go to seed. If the weeds are low, such as bindweed and spurge, scrape them off the soil. The timing of this task hinges on observation. The goal is to cut back just before the plant sets seed.

PUTTING UP BARRIERS Weed seeds are designed to travel. They tumble down streets and sidewalks; hitch rides on birds and lizards; and catch air currents. Barriers help block this constant migration. Whether a small wall, a tall fence, or vegetation, any type of barrier affects wind patterns and the places where weed seeds get deposited.

Whether 1 foot or 10 feet tall, vegetation is fantastic at pulling seeds and particulates out of the air. Some of the fire-resistant plants that would make great barriers to migrating seeds include ceanothus, cistus, justicia, rhus, salvia, santolina, teucrium, and westringia.

A low hedge of rosemary traps debris and weed seeds before they blow onto the property.

A small barrier can help reduce the amount of weed seeds being blown across a property. As wind rushes over a small wall, an eddy is created, causing the wind to circle in front of and behind the wall and deposit its debris and seeds.

PROTECTION

Providing protection helps stop weeds from either germinating or spreading. The techniques used to protect a landscape from weed seeds include planting aggressive plants, using weed fabrics, and laying mulches.

USE AGGRESSIVE PLANTS The best defense is often a strong offense. Using plants that can outcompete

Landscape fabric eventually becomes a nuisance. Unless it is biodegradable, it is often better to avoid weed-blocking fabric.

Common yarrow (*Achillea millefolium*) ia a fire-resistant aggressive spreader that can outcompete a variety of weeds.

weeds is one of the greatest time-savers in maintaining a landscape. The plants most likely to beat weeds have some of the characteristics below. Refer to the Lawn Alternatives table, page 62, for a list of aggressive plants.

- They trail and root across the top of the soil.

- They are self-repairing and spring back from injury.

- Their foliage blocks the sun from striking the soil.

- They may have aggressive roots near the surface that hog water and nutrients.

- They may be prolific seeders.

WEED FABRIC AND SIMILAR BARRIERS Cardboard, newspaper, plastic sheets, and weed fabric can be laid over soil to prevent underlying weeds from sprouting and new ones from taking root. Usually a thick layer of mulch is laid over these materials. Weed barriers such as this are effective in the short-term; however in the long-term these materials can increase maintenance costs.

MULCH Mulches provide incredible benefits: they can slow evaporation, suppress weeds, enrich the soil, reduce topsoil loss, increase rainwater infiltration, regulate soil temperature, and make an area look more attractive. But they can cause problems, too.

Not only can mulches be highly ignitable, but they can also disguise irrigation problems, alter the chemistry of the soil, shorten some plants' lives, and favor non-native weeds.

Below are the fundamentals of using mulches in fire country. They have been divided between inorganic and organic.

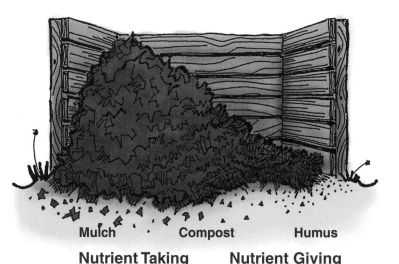

Mulch · **Compost** **Humus**
Nutrient Taking **Nutrient Giving**
Time and Levels of Decomposition

In fire country, avoid fine, dry, and ignitable mulches. These types of mulches include burlap sacks, cardboard, gorilla hair (redwood bark shavings), newspaper, sawdust, and straw. Less-flammable organic mulches include large-sized bark, cocoa hulls, compost, humus, manure, and tree clippings.

Inorganic Mulches

Inorganic mulches have grown in popularity because they are nonflammable, fairly inexpensive, and generally clean-looking. They are ideal for durable plants, such as scrub and desert plants. They require maintenance, although much less than most other land cover options do.

There are three broad categories of inorganic mulches: crushed aggregate (gravel), decomposed granite (commonly referred to as DG), and river rock. All three require weeding.

Organic Mulches

For purposes of simplicity, organic mulches can be categorized as either deterring or nourishing.

Deterring mulches are used to suppress weeds and are woody; high in carbon; and made from materials that are slow to decompose, such as camphor, eucalyptus, juniper, and pittosporum. Deterring mulches will initially rob the soil of nitrogen and are slow to give it back.

Nourishing mulches are used to support plant health. They are in a further state of decomposition and contain all kinds of helpful microorganisms and nutrients.

Important: Avoid using deterring and fine woody mulches within 10 feet of a structure—they are highly ignitable. Nourishing mulches, like humus, are not as dangerous and are preferred.

Fire-Safe Tips for Applying Mulch

Amount: To get all the benefits of mulch (water conservation, weed suppression), you will need at least a 2-inch layer; anything more than 4 inches is redundant. If a plant is prone to rot, keep mulch several inches away from its crown. Killing (smothering) the weeds already growing in an area requires a 6-inch layer of mulch.

Timing: Deterring mulches are generally needed no more than once a year. The best time to apply them is early winter, or just before weeds start taking off. Nourishing mulches may be needed twice a year. The best times to apply these are early spring, when plants need a blast of nutrients, and early fall, when the soil needs more protection from rain and runoff.

Irrigation and compaction: Lightly watering mulch around a structure will reduce ignitability, which is essential during fire weather. Regularly walking on mulch also helps reduce its flammability by reducing the amount of oxygen between pieces and increasing soil contact, which helps cool the mulch. However, both irrigation and compaction will reduce mulch's ability to suppress weeds.

ERADICATION

Removing weeds is never an easy task, and there is no easy way to do it. Refer to the next chapter, "Managing Wild Vegetation and Weeds," for all the ins and outs of effective weeding.

MAINTAINING EFFICIENT IRRIGATION

The goal of irrigation in fire country is to maintain adequate moisture levels without overirrigating. As a general rule, fire-retardant plants prefer shallow and frequent irrigation, while fire-resistant plants prefer deep and infrequent watering. Shallow and frequent irrigation means wetting the soil 2–5 inches deep, one to three times a week. Many lawn alternatives prefer this style of irrigation. Deep and infrequent means wetting the soil 6 inches–1.5 feet deep, once a week to once a month. Many of the trees and shrubs recommended in this book prefer this type of care.

While proper leaf moisture varies greatly between plants, any plant that is water stressed becomes far more ignitable.

Signs of water need:

- Wilting flowers, leaves, and stems

- Brittle (not limp) leaves

- Dull, bluish leaves

- Shedding of older leaves

- Burns around leaf edges

- Extensive leaf drop

- Stunted new growth

OVERIRRIGATION

Overirrigation leads to a variety of problems that lead to a more flammable landscape over the long haul. Problems caused by excess water include:

- Excess vegetative growth. This makes a plant prone to dieback if the water is turned down or stopped.

- Surface roots. Too much water pushes oxygen from the soil, and roots rise to

These *Aloe striata* plants are showing signs of water stress: shriveled leaves, dying older leaves, and stunted new growth.

the surface to breathe. These roots can become tripping hazards, suppress the growth of ground covers, and make the plant more prone to toppling.

- Increased humidity and heat. Wet soils store more solar radiation than dry soils. As the soil and air become hotter and more moist, the chance of fungus, disease, and pest problems increases.

Signs of overirrigation:

- Limp, drooping, or wilting flowers, leaves, and stems

- Edema (a blisterlike area on fleshy parts)

- Translucent or gray-hued leaves

- Irregular and rangy growth

- Persistent fungal infestations

- Lots of vegetative growth but little flowering or fruit

- A sour (not sweet) smell to the soil

CARING FOR HEDGES

Privacy is a vital human need, and as such, hedges are a dominant feature in residential communities. Unfortunately, hedges also create a fuel freeway and can lead a wildfire directly to a structure. Follow the guidelines below to maintain a less flammable hedge.

REPLACEMENT Any hedge with a dense, dead, and twiggy interior—full of highly ignitable material—must be removed and replanted. As a rule, expect to replace a hedge no less than every 12 years.

STAGGERED REPLACEMENT If your need for privacy is great, then remove and replant every third plant in the row, ensuring some degree of screening. The following year replace another third, and the year after that, the last third.

PRUNING Every other year, cut back about one-fifth of the plant's larger branches. The goal is twofold: First, deep pruning allows sunlight to strike the interior and encourages new growth from within the plant (shearing encourages growth on the outermost stems). Second, it allows you to reach in and pull and prune the dead material, which helps improve the plant's overall health, decrease pest problems, and reduce ignitability.

IRRIGATION Concentrating large plants together will cause the soil to dry quickly. Hedges generally need irrigation, which should be deep and infrequent; because fire-resistant hedge plants are broad-leaved and tough, shallow and frequent watering does not favor them. Deep and infrequent irrigation gets water at least 9 inches deep and then allows the soil to dry to that depth. This technique will reduce humidity and disease,

Manzanita as a hedge plant is fire resistant and low maintenance, and its interior is fairly open and easy to clean.

encourage a soil's exchange of gases, and slow but not compromise a plant's growth, extending its useful life.

FERTILIZATION Fertilization will probably be necessary, but it must be done with discretion. Too much will spur rapid plant growth, might increase pest problems, and increases maintenance costs. Organic fertilizers are recommended because of their lower overall nutrient values: they give a little over a long time. Nothing more than compost or humus may be needed for native plants. Plants demanding higher nutrients can rely on blood meal (nitrogen), bone meal (phosphorus), and wood ash (potassium). Notably, urban soils are generally not deficient in phosphorus or potassium.

WASH FOLIAGE Hedges trap anything floating in air currents. This debris and dust coats the surface of leaves and reduces their ability to breathe and photosynthesize, causing pest infestations and dieback, and ultimately increasing flammability. Washing foliage will increase plant health and reduce the amount of ignitable wood. Hedges along roads need more frequent washing.

MANAGING TERRACES

Terracing a slope is a great way to break up its length and create a safer environment. But terracing can cause problems too, and they demand maintenance.

One of the biggest problems caused by terracing is erosion. The terracing structure's face catches rainfall and jettisons it with concentrated force that causes erosion not only at the foot of the structure but also farther downslope. All terracing structures have this problem—stacked walls, staked boards and logs, and even berms can create sheeting water and erosion problems.

MAINTENANCE RECOMMENDATIONS

- Maintain a low-growing shrub at the foot of the structure to buffer it from rainfall and irrigation and stabilize the soil.

The impermeable face of terracing structures causes runoff and erosion. This sheeting water undermines the foot of a structure and can increase topsoil loss farther downslope.

Some of the ways to protect terracing structures from erosion are tumbling plants, riprap, and small shrubs.

- Maintain low-growing plants that can cascade over the face of the structure, buffering it from the rain and irrigation.

- Stack riprap at the foot of the structure to diffuse sheeting runoff.

- Once a year, haul the soil back up to the foot of the structure and compact it.

CHAPTER 18
MANAGING WILD VEGETATION AND WEEDS

The secret to reducing the threat of fire is to mimic the effects of fire. Wildfires can be beneficial: They remove dead, dying, and diseased plants. They devour plant-consuming insects and pathogens. They nourish the soil while reducing nitrogen, an unwanted byproduct of burning fossil fuels. And fire rejuvenates many wildflowers, perennials, and shrubs. The biggest challenge for people living in fire country is to become that fire—to clean, nourish, and rejuvenate the landscape around their homes.

Removal and replanting is a natural process, and our labor replaces fire as the dominant agent of change. This chapter provides the basics of fuel reduction, land reclamation, and protecting wildlife.

Above: Reducing the severity of a wildfire in a wild landscape is complicated. The needs of the native fauna and flora are as important as those of the human inhabitants. **Top:** This photo illustrates a common problem: too much weed whacking over too many years has led to an old and flammable forest. All the young sprouts that would have eventually become the new forest have been routinely chopped. Refer to page 109 for tips on working with the ecology of your site. Photographed by Adam Rowe

Thick coveralls, a face mask, gloves, and sturdy boots mean this individual is serious about personal safety. A fire extinguisher and a board on which to lay hot equipment mean he is also serious about fire safety.

TECHNIQUES TO REDUCE FUELS ON NATURALLY OCCURRING LANDSCAPES

Managing fuels on naturally occurring landscapes demands different techniques. The primary goals in these landscapes are fuel reduction and erosion control. Because of this, the plants that can live under the blades of a string trimmer (no taller than 4–9 inches) should be actively encouraged. These plants help stabilize soil. Actively selecting for naturally occurring, low-growing plants means mowing or chopping the area only after these plants have set seed, ensuring good coverage year after year.

GENERAL GUIDELINES FOR WEEDING AND RECLAIMING LANDSCAPES

Before renting a tiller or buying herbicides, consider these general guidelines about the processes of removing vegetation, clearing land, and reclamation.

PERSONAL SAFETY From small nicks and insect bites to gaping wounds and sprains, clearing land is not only physical, but also involves the use of dangerous equipment. Always wear eye and ear protection when using string trimmers, chainsaws, and chippers. Always wear ankle-high boots, thick pants, a long-sleeved shirt, and gloves, and take regular hydration breaks to reduce fatigue and injury.

MODERATION Trying to tackle too much at one time can lead to a variety of problems. Erosion, an invasion of weeds, storm damage, and even personal injury are common when quality is sacrificed for quantity. Important: Never clear more than can be replanted in one season, especially on slopes. Also stagger the removal of shrubs and trees in dense groves. Taking too much of the grove out at one time makes damage from wind, freezing temperatures, and sun more likely. Selectively remove no more than 30% of a plant or grove at a time, planning to come back in two years to remove another 30%.

EQUIPMENT One of the biggest and most persistent causes of wildfires is equipment use. Mowers, string trimmers, and chainsaws, along with many other machines, are a constant source of friction, heat, and sparks.

To avoid starting a fire while working with machinery, take the following precautions:

- Put spark arresters on all exhaust ports, and repair holes in existing systems and arresters.

- Check for a buildup of carbon in the exhaust system and on spark plugs.

- Refuel only when the engine has cooled.

- Never lay a running or hot engine in grass or other ignitable vegetation.

- Bring a fire extinguisher to the work site.

- Avoid working past 10 a.m. during the fire season.

- Avoid all work that involves machinery during extreme fire-weather conditions—hot, dry, windy days.

TIMING Never clear fuels during fire weather. Late winter and early spring are the best times to clear landscapes: most weeds have yet to set seed, most plants will recover from injury, and the soil is easy to work in. Clearing land after the threat of fire has passed—late fall and early winter—is not advised, and clearing land just before the start of the rains significantly increases the chances of topsoil loss.

ECOLOGY Everything coexists in a garden—bacteria and bugs, plants and animals—everything, including us. Take great care to protect these vital residents when weeding. Protect plants from falling and dragged debris. Lay boards and plywood over beds, grasses, and soils to distribute the weight of repeated footsteps. If working in dry conditions, lightly water to help bind the soil and reduce topsoil loss. And never work in wet soils because of the oxygen-removing compaction it causes. Refer to the section at the end of this chapter (page 109) for a deeper discussion.

HERBICIDES All pesticides should be well understood and used with care. More often than not, unwanted vegetation will have to be removed by hand, and killing plants prior to pulling makes the task harder. Legally, you must read an herbicide's label before using.

LAND RECLAMATION

Simply put, land reclamation involves transforming a naturally occurring landscape into one with specific plants, whether those plants are native or not. Land can be reclaimed from invasive grasses and transformed to native scrub plants, or native scrub plants can be transformed to fire-resistant, hill-holding ornamental ground covers.

Reclamation is never a one-time event. Clearing is only the first step. A landscape cleared but not reclaimed can quickly reestablish itself within 2–5 years. A successful job of reclamation will include the steps below.

1. Remove existing unwanted plants.

2. Exhaust the soil of its unwanted propagules (seeds and vegetative starts).

Continued on page 109

TECHNIQUES FOR MANAGING FUELS IN WILD AND NATURALLY OCCURRING LANDSCAPES

TECHNIQUE	TOOLS	PLANTS	TIMING	NOTES
Controlled burns	Fire personnel and their equipment	All plants: annuals to shrubs and around trees	Controlled burns should only occur with a predetermined prescription of ideal plant moisture, air temperature, humidity, and wind.	Refer to the section on controlled burns in Chapter 11.
Chopping/ mowing	Machetes, sickles, and machine-powered string trimmers and brush cutters	Any plant with a trunk diameter of an inch or less	Preferably before the unwanted plant has set seed. This technique produces sparks and should never be used in fire weather.	One of the most common techniques for reducing fuels
Cutting	Chainsaws, pruners, and saws	Trees and large shrubs	Large disruptions should be timed to minimize erosion and maximize healing: typically late winter and early spring	Often used in conjunction with herbicides for resprouting plants
Digging	Shovels and hand trowels	Ground covers and shrubs	Preferably late winter–spring, giving ample time for recovery	Digging excites many seeds to sprout, and follow-up is needed.
Grazing	Cattle, goats, and sheep	Grasses, forbs, some woody ground covers, shrubs, and low branches on trees	Year-round, except in areas with erosion risk and then late winter–early summer	Cow and sheep prefer grasses and forbs. Goats prefer broadleaf plants to 4 ft. high.
Herbicides	Typically non-selective, translocated with dye added, applied with either pump-sprayer or sponge	Applied on either leaves less than 5 ft. high or just-cut stumps of larger plants; good for monocultures	Timing varies; read the instructions for the best results.	Physically, it is the least intrusive, but the long-term biological and cultural costs can be significant.
Plowing/tilling	Shovels, rototillers, and tractors	Best with fleshy plants, like annuals, biennials, perennials, and young shrubs and trees	Preferably before plants set seed	Tilling multiple times may be necessary to exhaust the soil of propagules. Too much tilling will reduce soil fertility and raise pH.
Pulling	Hands, strong back, and weed wrench	Anything smaller than a small shrub can be pulled; anything larger requires digging.	Preferably late winter/early spring, before plant sets seed and allowing recovery time before rains	Made much easier with pliable soil
Scrapping	Hand hoes and bulldozer	Any type of plant lower than the blade of the scrapper.	Anytime but during fire weather—this method of control will produce sparks.	Common on trails and dirt roads; usually removes some of the topsoil
Solarization	Clear or black plastic	Young plants, no more than 6 in. high.	Anytime, but works faster in summer. Solarization takes about 4 months.	Has the potential to kill everything, bad and good; also creates a big plastic-trash problem

HANDLING WEED WASTE

Removing unwanted plants in fire country often means managing large masses of woody debris. There are four ways to handle weed waste: compost, burn, haul away, or bioutilization.

Composting is an inexpensive method, but it requires the most time and space. Weed waste needs the most extensive type of composting to ensure that the vegetative starts and seeds are dead. A site's ability to properly compost also hinges on its ability to use the product; there is little point to composting if it will not be used.

Burning is the quickest and least expensive method, but it is not legal in urban areas throughout the nation. Burning used to be the most common method of disposal, but a region's air quality and public health mandates dictate a wiser approach.

Hauling the debris is the most expensive method of removal, but it is the quickest, by far. The expense of hauling is related to weight and size, both of which will shrink if the pile is spread out and allowed to dry before hauling. Hauling is the method that can lead to landfilling.

Bioutilization strives to use the vegetative waste. Some of the things greenwaste can get turned into include mulch, products such as pallets, and energy generation. While a residential property owner may not have the means to efficiently repurpose greenwaste, a municipality handling thousands of tons of greenwaste might. See Bioutilization, page 132, for more detail.

3. Plant preferred plants.

4. Possibly irrigate new plants.

5. Weed.

6. Control topsoil loss until new plants provide cover.

7. Weed.

8. Slow the migration of weed starts from neighboring properties.

9. Weed.

Reclamation is more extensive and expensive than simply reducing plant fuels. Reclaiming a landscape in urban areas is easier than in the wildlands. Landscapes that border open space have to contend with a greater number of weed seeds, wildlife, and unpredictable events, such as infestations and droughts. Land reclamation in urban areas may take 2–4 years; reclamation in rural areas can take up to 5–7 years.

WORKING WITH THE ECOLOGY OF YOUR SITE

Earth is losing species at a rate comparable to only six other times in the planet's history—we are experiencing a modern-day extinction event. In order to remove plants, clear land, and reclaim land in such a way as to reduce the harmful impacts, make sure you follow the guidelines below.

BE AWARE OF BREEDING SEASONS There is no ideal time to disrupt habitat. However, nothing is more damaging than working during the breeding season. Whether bee, butterfly, bird, or fox, animals caring for offspring are particularly vulnerable. Get to know the species you are trying to protect. For instance, if managing the landscape for spring nesting birds, such as scrub jays, then weed whacking may have to wait until early summer. On the other hand, if managing summer nesting birds, such as goldfinches, then avoid land clearing late spring–summer.

Above: This area was completely cleared eight months ago. The mustard plants are new seedlings inspired by a late-spring rain and sun. If this area is not weeded again, the mustard will have a chance to produce seed, extending the process of reclamation for another couple of years. **Below:** Clearing land does not have to be a draconian exercise. We can leave room for ecological health and vitality. Maintaining islands of untouched vegetation helps ecological processes better recover from the disturbance.

USE HERBICIDES RESPONSIBLY The advantages of herbicides are ease of use, quick and inexpensive treatment, and low site disturbance. The disadvantages are its toxicity and impacts on food chains, biological viability, and overall species diversity. Insects and birds are susceptible to the effects of toxins. If herbicides must be used, follow these tips:

- Apply only when there is no wind.

- Apply at night when most species are least active.

- Read the directions (required by law), mix the proper amounts, and apply at the optimum time of year.

- Do the research: there are many chemical options, and all have varying degrees of toxicity and persistence.

LEAVE A LITTLE DEAD STUFF Dead material is essential to ecological health. Piles of dead material provide nesting opportunities as well as nesting material and food (mostly in the form of insects) for a wide variety of wildland species. Dead material should never be allowed in Zone 1, but if Zone 2 is fairly flat and well maintained, small piles of habitat-helping debris will not hurt.

CLEAR A LITTLE AT A TIME Try not to clear more than one-third of an area at a time, always leaving two-thirds untouched. The unaffected areas provide refuge for fleeing insects and animals while providing the seeds and vegetative starts that will reinhabit the site and hold the topsoil. Clear another third of the area the following year, and so forth.

LEAVE ISLANDS If an entire area must be mowed at one time, then try to leave islands of untouched vegetation. These islands are a refuge, a storehouse for propagules, and a source of food until the nearby landscape recovers. The islands should be no less than 15 feet wide, with another island not less than 30 feet away. These islands are also where forests and groves regenerate.

POSTFIRE RECOVERY: CONTROLLING EROSION

CHAPTER 19
FIRST AID FOR FIRE-SCARRED LANDSCAPES

You are battered and fatigued, but the fight to save your property and community is far from over. Erosion leaps as high as 200% following wildfires in urban-influenced landscapes. With this increase comes mass sedimentation and alteration of streambeds, property, and infrastructure.

THE PROBLEM

Fires eliminate tree canopies, burn off leaf litter, and expose the soil. Then, when there is nothing to slow or stop them, wind and water gain leverage and soil gets shoved around as a consequence.

But the problem is not just the lack of protective cover. Recently burned landscapes also have to contend with repellency. Fires cook the natural waxes in the soils. When these waxes cool, they coat the first inch of soil with a repellency layer, stopping water from infiltrating.

The consequences can be dire when the lack of protective cover and repellency are combined. Fire-scarred communities can produce incredible amounts of runoff and debris flow, which can overwhelm drainage systems, leading to extensive erosion elsewhere. Worse still, debris flowing down slopes can overrun homes, businesses, and small communities. These types of events can and have led to personal injury and death.

Above: Debris and mudflows endanger people, private property, and public infrastructure.

REPELLENCY LAYER

A water repellency (hydrophobic) layer is created when a fire melts waxes and resins found naturally in soils. The melted resins turn into a gas, rise, and then cool and condense on top of soil, coating it with an impermeable layer.

When rain hits a repellency layer, it quickly runs off. As water runs, its power grows, and its ability to move things, like soil particles, grows proportionally. Hydrophobic soils are prone to topsoil loss and can produce severe debris flows.

Lightly watering an injured landscape can help break the repellency layer. If repellency persists after multiple light waterings, then you will have to physically break

This puddle of water has been sitting on the sandy soil for over 5 minutes. A repellency layer has stopped it from infiltrating. Repellency is more common in sandy soils that grow resinous plants.

the barrier. Grass rakes, hoes, and Hula Ho weeders (also called stirrup hoes) can be lightly dragged across the top of the soil to break the repellency layer.

Although most soils lose their repellency within a year, some may stay hydrophobic for up to six years. The amount of water repellency a fire creates is related to the fire's intensity and the size of a soil's particles. Larger soil particles, such as sand, will have greater rates of repellency.

IMMEDIATE FIRST AID

A well-planned and quick response to the threat of erosion is needed. Below are the first five things that must be done after a wildfire. These steps will dramatically reduce a site's chances of stormwater runoff and topsoil loss.

The first five steps are drain rainwater, divert sheeting rainwater, reduce traffic on the injured landscape, irrigate, and leave the fallen debris and mess.

1. DRAIN RAINWATER

Drainage systems will be clogged with debris after a fire. Water skipping out of drains, such as swales, is a leading cause of erosion, fire or not. Roof gutters, street gutters, culverts, swales, infiltration and detention basins, small streams, and concrete waterways will need cleaning.

2. DIVERT SHEETING WATER

The chances of topsoil loss dramatically rise if a landscape receives sheeting water from nearby features. Driveways, roadways, sidewalks, and parking lots are often designed to sheet their runoff to the landscape. If this is the case on your property, divert that runoff away from the landscape and toward the storm drain system.

RUNOFF DIVERSION DEVICES

	DESCRIPTION	COSTS	EFFECTIVENESS	LONGEVITY	MAINTENANCE
Bales	Oat, barley, wheat, and rice straw bales used to depower and divert runoff and sediment. They are used along roads, the base of slopes, and around the perimeter of structures.	Inexpensive and quickly placed and staked	Good at diverting and depowering low to medium flows	Short-term remedy; typically pulled up and composted after the threat of rain has passed because they become a fire hazard and a habitat for unwanted animals if left in place	Very low maintenance
Check dams	Staked boards running mostly perpendicular to the flow of runoff. These small walls are used to both divert and slow runoff. The boards are generally 4 ft. long, 9 in. wide, and ½ in. thick; 2-ft. stakes made from #3 rebar are used to keep the boards in place.	Inexpensive and quickly built	Effective for low–moderate flows only	Rarely last longer than 3 years, less if they manage regular flows; will eventually fail by either getting pushed over or having the uphill side fill with debris and sediment	Keep the uphill side clean to reduce pressure and increase longevity.
Diversion ditches	Quickly dug to transport water away from a vulnerable area; generally 6 in.–1.5 ft. deep and 1.5–3 ft. wide	Quickly dug with no material costs	Suitable only for low–moderate flows; anything more leads to rapid deterioration.	Short-term solution. If not lined with river rock or planted, then it will degrade within 2 years.	Require maintenance to retain shape during rains; generally turned into concrete ditches, dry creeks, or swales. Refer to the next chapter.
Dry stacked walls	Made from rock, broken concrete, bricks, and even roof tiles and used to divert, direct, and depower runoff; usually short and running mostly perpendicular to a slope or water path. Gravity, as opposed to concrete, holds them together.	Labor-intensive, but the materials are generally inexpensive.	Can be built to withstand low–high flows; not as effective as sandbags, but longer-lasting and more aesthetically appealing	Can be long-lasting if built with care	Two types of problems occur with these walls. First, dirt and debris will collect on the upslope side, reducing water-holding and -slowing capacity while increasing pressure on the structure; remove this accumulation every 2–4 years. Second, the downward side of the wall will erode, eventually undermining it; every 2–3 years pull the soil back up to the wall and either plant to stabilize or compact it. Refer to Terracing (page 122) for more detail.
Sandbags	Mostly impermeable small walls made from bags filled with sand, aggregate, or soil; laid and compacted in a running-bond pattern	Material costs are inexpensive, but labor costs can be high.	Very effective in the short term for low–high flows	Good for 2 years, but the bag's hemp or plastic weave deteriorates rapidly after that.	After 2 years they need to be replaced with a permanent solution.

Dry stacked walls are inexpensive, quick to construct, and typically made from local materials, such as river rock and broken concrete.

These staked boards direct sheeting mud and water away from the hiking path.

Straw bales divert, slow, and filter sheeting water and runoff. They are also inexpensive and quick to use. Their only drawback is their flammability—straw bales are a short-term fix only.

3. MINIMIZE TRAFFIC

Keep foot and equipment traffic off burned landscapes. Activity on slopes will increase the likelihood of erosion by weakening a soil's bonds, dislodging soil particles, and trampling just-sprouted plants. Activity on flat ground can compact the soil and lower the rate of water absorption, increasing runoff.

Instead, plan on working on an injured landscape only after a plan of restoration has been developed and all the materials and tools are ready for use.

4. WATERING

A recently burned landscape will absolutely need water, but there are two distinct types. The first immediate watering is aimed at breaking the soil's repellency layer. This watering is light—no more than 1 gallon per 10 square feet. The goal here is to water only the top ¼ inch of soil.

Once the repellency layer has been broken, you can begin deeper waterings. The goal is to get the water

Rainfall

Activity

Slope

Debris

Soil

Length and Severity of Fire

The somewhat predictable chance of water runoff and topsoil loss is influenced by six factors: length and steepness of the slope, amount of rain, type of vegetation burned, type of soil, amount of animal and human activity, and severity of the fire.

Leaving charred debris in place helps prevent erosion and protect surviving seeds until a restoration plan has been developed.

4 inches deep and encourage seeds, roots, and surviving plants to sprout. Three to 5 gallons of water per 10 square feet will be required. Water again only when the first 2 inches have dried.

5. LEAVE THE MESS

Do not clean your landscape—the debris on your injured site provides much-needed protection. The charred remains of plants and garden features protect the landscape from wind and water erosion, slow sheeting water, and help prevent the surviving seeds and plants from drying out. Do not remove debris until a restoration plan has been developed.

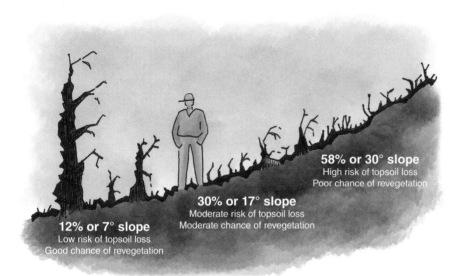

58% or 30° slope
High risk of topsoil loss
Poor chance of revegetation

30% or 17° slope
Moderate risk of topsoil loss
Moderate chance of revegetation

12% or 7° slope
Low risk of topsoil loss
Good chance of revegetation

Various parts of a slope will score differently and, consequently, call for different methods of erosion control. Refer to the next chapter for methods of diverting and depowering rainfall and runoff for the various levels of erosion risk.

ASSESS YOUR RISK OF TOPSOIL LOSS

Determining the levels of erosion risk helps not only prioritize recovery resources but also determine the aggressiveness of your response. The erosion test below provides indicators as to the likelihood of topsoil loss, but for an accurate analysis of risk, consult a local Certified Professional in Erosion and Sediment Control (CPESC).

The somewhat predictable chance of water runoff and topsoil loss is influenced by six factors: length and steepness of a slope, amount of rain, type of vegetation burned, type of soil, amount of activity by animals and humans, and severity of the fire. Go through the list of contributing factors, mark the box that best describes your landscape, and add the points together. The tallied score corresponds to an approximate level of erosion risk. Importantly, different parts of a landscape will score differently—always prioritize work around the areas with the highest risk.

This test was developed in February 1996, following the October 1995 Vision Fire in Point Reyes and Inverness, California. It was developed in partnership with Robert Crowell of Cagwin and Dorward, a landscape architecture and engineering firm in San Rafael. This test is a fire-modified version of the Universal Soil Loss Equation, a nationwide standard developed for farmers. It gauges the likelihood of topsoil loss only, not of landslides or soil slips.

SLOPE

A slope's degree of incline has the greatest influence on its chances of producing erosion. The incline and length of a slope are two measurable factors. See page 51 for a method of determining your degree of slope.

Although slopes have a higher risk of erosion, flat ground is susceptible too. Scorched and bare landscapes are easily compacted and prone to puddling and sheeting water, contributing to erosion elsewhere.

STEEPNESS OF SLOPE

1 Point	0–16%	Not likely
2 Points	17%–34%	Low likelihood
4 Points	35%–51%	Likely
8 Points	52% and up	Most likely

LENGTH OF SLOPE

1 Point	0–25 feet
2 Point	26–50 feet
4 Points	51–100 feet
8 Points	101–200 feet

RAIN

How a burned landscape reacts to storms depends on the time between the fire and the first rain and on the rain's intensity and duration. Plan on heavy autumn and winter downpours when determining chance of erosion.

RAIN

1 Point	A late autumn sprinkle with light to moderate storms through the remaining season
2 Points	Late autumn sprinkle with heavy winter downpour
4 Points	No autumn rain and heavy winter downpour
6 Points	Heavy early autumn and winter downpour

TYPE AND DENSITY OF PLANTS BURNED

This is a forest-vs.-grasslands comparison. You are looking at two measures: the amount of debris involved and the amount of plants remaining that can resprout.

TYPE AND DENSITY

1 Point	Formerly densely forested land. Trees had shrubs and possibly ground covers growing below them.
2 Points	Formerly a landscape with scattered trees and no understory shrubs, or a landscape with only shrubs and ground covers. Oak woodland and coastal scrub communities are examples.
3 Points	Formerly grassy with scattered perennials.
4 Points	Formerly a landscape with tough and difficult growing conditions. Plants are shallow rooted, sprawling, and sparsely planted.

TYPE OF SOIL

The structure, density, and size of a soil's particles influence its likelihood of erosion. Clay soils are the least erodible; sand and gravel are the most. But clay soils have other problems: They are much faster to produce runoff due to poor infiltration, and this leads to the washing away of fine particles and the siltation of streams. Sand and gravel do not travel like clay.

SOIL

1 Point	A clay-dominant soil with silt, sand, and/or organic matter
2 Points	A sandy soil mixed with silt and organic matter
3 Points	A clay soil with little or no organic matter
6 Points	Sandy soils with little or no organic material; loose and gravelly rock

Gopher activity contributes to erosion.

AMOUNT AND TYPE OF ACTIVITY

Activity by animals and humans has a large impact on the chance of topsoil loss—the more activity, the more erosion. Tunneling animals, such as gophers and ground squirrels, are a threat to stability, more so if the fire has displaced their predators. Even walking on a burned landscape can slow its recovery; trampling lowers germinations rates, redistributes seeds, and crushes new seedlings.

ACTIVITY

1 Point	Animals and people walking on the site
3 Points	Storm drains and gutters clogged; tunneling and browsing animals lacking predators and with large populations
4 Points	An area that was cleared before the fire and never replanted, allowing shallow-rooted opportunists to grow
6 Points	A barren landscape; also, massive cuts into a hill and/or fill brought in on a slope

FIRE INTENSITY

A low-temperature fire can cleanse and awaken a dynamic landscape. A high-temperature fire will do just the opposite—not much survives 2,000°F. Fire intensity affects not only a landscape's rate of recovery but also the amount of repellency a soil has. Hotter fires produce more repellency. This test assumes a fairly hot fire, slow recovery, and high repellency.

OFF–SITE WATER

Roadways, sidewalks, driveways, and parking lots can deposit their runoff on surrounding properties. If your burned landscape is receiving sheeting water, the risk of erosion is high.

OFF-SITE WATER

0 Points	Slope not receiving sheeting water from elsewhere
6 Points	Slope receiving sheeting water from elsewhere

APPROXIMATE LEVEL OF RISK

RISK

6–13 points	Fairly low risk of erosion
14–20 points	Medium risk of erosion
21–28 points	Fairly high risk of erosion
29–44 points	High risk of erosion

CHAPTER 20
HOLDING YOUR HILL: LONG-TERM RECOVERY

In native landscapes, topsoil loss and soil slips can be forces that spur succession and diversity. In domestic and natural landscapes, just the opposite is true: erosion leads only to cost and harm. Covered below are the design and maintenance strategies for managing sloped properties in and around urban areas.

Organized around the goals of diverting and depowering runoff, this section includes the most effective strategies for holding your hill.

DIVERTING RUNOFF

The first step in protecting a slope is to make sure that sheeting water (runoff) is diverted away from the risky areas. The previous chapter highlighted short-term diversion strategies (bales, check dams, diversion ditches, and sandbags) and longer-term strategies (dry stacked walls). This section provides more permanent solutions.

TECHNIQUES AND DEVICES

Covered below are descriptions and maintenance requirements for three permanent diversion devices: concrete ditches, dry creeks, and swales.

Concrete Ditches
Description: Concrete ditches are constructed to run along the face of a slope and catch its sheeting water. They are expensive but vital on steep slopes.

Above: Hoping to depower runoff and topsoil loss, land managers laid jute matting over this high-risk area.

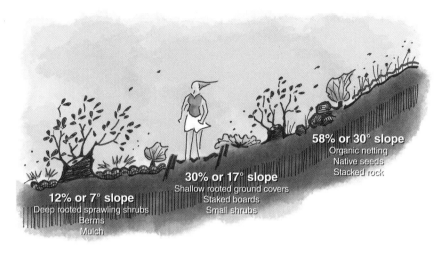

Erosion remedies are as varied as the landscape. Encourage any plants that have survived and sprouted, using a method appropriate for your particular slope.

58% or 30° slope
Organic netting
Native seeds
Stacked rock

30% or 17° slope
Shallow rooted ground covers
Staked boards
Small shrubs

12% or 7° slope
Deep rooted sprawling shrubs
Berms
Mulch

Swales

Description: These are simply ditches that have been planted. The plants reduce the likelihood of collapse and scouring. Swales are effective not only for diverting and depowering runoff but also for removing debris, sediment, and toxins from runoff.

Maintenance: Any earthen feature needs regular maintenance. Accumulated sediment needs to be hauled out; vegetation needs to be thinned and cleaned; and the walls of the swale may need to be shored up.

Maintenance: Water skipping out of devices like these is the leading cause of erosion—fire or not. Concrete waterways need annual cleaning to remove the debris and sediment that would allow water to skip out. Sometimes the downhill side of these ditches erodes away, and maintenance is needed bring the soil back up. The downhill side can also be protected by small shrubs and stacked riprap.

Dry Creeks

Description: Dry creeks are large ditches lined with rock. They are constructed to divert, drain, and depower rainwater and runoff. They are generally inexpensive and aesthetically pleasing.

Maintenance: While this device is generally low maintenance, it does have a couple of problems. First, weeds will inevitably grow between the rocks, and reaching in and around rocks to remove weeds is time-consuming. Herbicides, vinegar, and flaming are options of control (although flaming is only good if the rock is more than 6 inches deep and there is no leafy debris). The second problem is the accumulation of debris and sediment. Vacuuming and blowing the accumulation will delay the eventual task of digging up the rock, removing the sediment, and resetting everything.

Dry creeks, used to divert and depower runoff, are generally low maintenance, but they do need to be weeded and cleaned of debris regularly.

DEPOWERING RUNOFF

Depowering runoff and rainfall reduces its ability to cause erosion and damage. Depowering devices can be categorized as either mechanical or horticultural.

MECHANICAL REMEDIES

After the immediate first aid of a fire-scarred slope, it is time to employ longer-term strategies. These strategies, covered below, include fiber rolls, microbasins, mulch, organic matting, and terracing.

Note: If managing erosion risk and runoff in dry/desert landscapes, refer to Brad Lancaster's book *Rainwater Harvesting for Drylands and Beyond: Guiding Principles to Welcome Rain into Your Life and Landscape* for effective and nourishing landscaping tips.

Fiber Rolls

Description: Fiber rolls are straw, rice hulls, or coconut waste bound by strong plastic mesh. They depower runoff and help screen its debris and sediment. Fiber rolls are used across slopes, perpendicular in swales, and around storm drains. They are good for slowing low to medium flows of runoff.

Maintenance: Fiber rolls degrade within one or two years, and the plastic netting should be removed from the landscape.

This slope has a high chance of topsoil loss. Wildfire landscapers sprayed hydromulch, dug in fiber rolls, and tried to work around resprouting shrubs. Combined, these three strategies have been effective at depowering rainfall.

Microbasins

Description: Microbasins are simply small depressions dug into a slope. They are quick to construct and effective on flat to medium-steep slopes. They are used to depower runoff and increase infiltration.

Maintenance: Over time these basins will fill with dirt and debris. Regrading will be necessary every 1–3 years.

Mulch

Description: Woody chipped material is often used to depower sheeting runoff. Without matting or netting, mulch helps slopes with a low risk of erosion; with matting and netting, it helps medium-risk slopes. Unfortunately, mulch is not always the best remedy. It can suppress the growth of soil-holding weeds and increase a soil's amount of nutrients, which may encourage unwanted weeds instead of native plants. Mulch is best used in urban landscapes, rather than natural or native ones.

Maintenance: For mulch to be effective, it must retain its depth. If woody mulch is supposed to be 4 inches thick, then replace it when it loses 50% (2 inches), refilling back to 4 inches. Never add more than the prescription, which in this example is 4 inches. *Important:* Avoid using coarse, woody, and dry mulches within 10 feet of a structure.

Organic Matting

Description: An organic net that lays over the soil, like jute matting, this erosion-control method is used on slopes with low to medium risk of topsoil loss. Organic matting helps not only hold the topsoil but also depower runoff, increase infiltration rates, and spur revegetating efforts.

Maintenance: Organic matting will break down, if not decompose, within two years.

Terracing

Description: Terracing is a small wall that depends on a cut or fill. Terraces break up the length of a slope, slowing topsoil loss, depowering runoff, and increasing water infiltration.

Maintenance: Terraces are generally low maintenance. In fact, cutting and leveling small portions of a hill creates stable places to walk and work and can reduce maintenance costs. However, the downslope side of the wall will erode, eventually undermining it. Every 2–3 years the soil will have to be pulled back up to the wall and either compacted or planted to stabilize the soil and footing. Refer to Chapter 10 ("Slopes") or Chapter 17 ("Maintaining Zones 1 and 2") for maintenance recommendations.

Terracing is a fantastic strategy in fire country. It allows for more moisture penetration and, consequently, a greater range of plants to be grown. Terracing also allows a landscape to be used more, which inherently lowers its flammability.

EXTREME MEASURES

Some slopes are simply too unstable and need more aggressive measures than what is offered below. If your landscape tested for a high likelihood of topsoil loss, then you might have to stabilize it with either wire matting or plastic sheeting. You will definitely have to call a Certified Professional Soil Erosion and Sediment Control Specialist. Importantly, avoid any unnecessary work on the slope: activity increases instability.

Chain-link matting: Rolled out down a slope and anchored with stakes, wire netting helps hold a slope's loose topsoil. It is also used to hold back tumbling rocks. Wire matting works well with seeding.

Plastic sheeting: Rolled out down a slope and anchored with sandbags and stakes, plastic sheeting prevents rain from striking a slope and dislodging topsoil. Extensive measures are needed at the toe of these slopes to handle the large volume of fast-moving runoff.

HORTICULTURAL REMEDIES

Included in this section are options such as living with weeds, seeding, hydroseeding, and planting, which includes tips on plant selection and how to plant.

Living with Wild Vegetation and Weeds

Weeds occupy the same places people do. We have such a unique and enduring impact on the landscape that large groups of plants have evolved to thrive in just those conditions. In fact, many weeds are formally classified as foot-followers. Battling weeds is battling a part of our nature.

Weeds will help control topsoil loss. Managers of large properties have learned how to live peacefully with naturally occurring vegetation. They've learned how to manage a weedy landscape's fuel. Anything lower than the blade of a string trimmer is encouraged to thrive; islands of vegetation are left untouched (to help recolonize cleared areas); and old and spindly trees are removed, while just-sprouted volunteers are encouraged. A good land manager is conscience of both fuel reduction and regrowth.

Seeding

Seeding a fire-scarred landscape to reduce topsoil loss is a common remedy. Seeding, however, has as many disadvantages as advantages.

Seeding's advantages are low site disturbance and providing quick cover for relatively low cost. And if a slope has irrigation, chances of controlling topsoil loss are good. Some of the disadvantages are smothering native plants, suppressing better-adapted weeds, seeded plants migrating to native landscapes, and creating flash fuels the following summer.

Seeding should be done on slopes with a medium or high chance of topsoil loss. Areas with a low risk should opt for planting, a preferred strategy. Seeding is a temporary solution. If longer-lived perennials and small shrubs are not encouraged, whether through planting or volunteers, then the risk of soil slips and landslides will be greater 4–7 years after a fire as the burned landscape's roots decompose and the seeded plants' population declines.

SELECTING SEEDS

Choosing the right type of seeds for erosion control is a horticultural art. Typically, seeds are grasses (annual or perennial), wildflowers (annual, biennial, and perennial), and perennials. Shrubs, succulents, and vines are not seeded. What type of seed is best for your slope hinges on these five factors:

1. **Amount of irrigation**. Irrigated landscapes can grow a greater range of seed plants than unirrigated ones.

2. **Slope aspect**. The direction your slope faces influences the type of seed selected and its chance of germination. Seed plants for south-facing slopes are different than those for north-facing slopes.

3. **Degree of slope.** Steep slopes are tough to irrigate, tough to seed, and tough to establish— only the toughest plants will do. Moderate slopes can grow a wider range.

4. **Depth of topsoil.** Slopes with topsoil that is 2 inches deep or more can grow a much greater variety of seed plants than a slope with only ½ inch of topsoil.

5. **Chance of seed plants migrating to open spaces.** If your property is close to a native landscape, such as a state or federal park, then choosing seeds that will not become a weed on those lands is essential.

Picking the right seed for your risky slope is regionally determined. Experts in your community know the right type of seed based on the factors above. If you need to seed, get a list from your local nursery, Resource Conservation District (RCD), or native plant society.

INITIAL IRRIGATION Although not always possible, irrigating an area several days prior to seeding improves chances of success. Water will help break a repellency layer and recharge a soil and its microbes. The goal is to get the water about 3 inches deep. The soil should be only slightly moist when seeding. If soil sticks to the bottom of your boots, it is too wet to seed.

Slopes without irrigation will have to wait for the rains to sow. Seeds are cast after or during the second rain of the season, allowing the first rain to break a soil's repellency and recharge the soil. Seeds require 6–14 days of moist soil to sprout. If the time between sowing the seeds and the rain is longer than a month, then the area may have to be seeded again.

SOWING SEEDS ON A SLOPE Sowing seeds should be done only after all other devices to divert, drain, and depower water have been installed. At the very least, runoff must be diverted away from the area to be seeded. Follow the steps below to seed a recently burned landscape.

RAKING Scarring the ground before sowing seeds has several benefits. Raking breaks the water repellency layer, removes the larger debris that would inhibit germination, and mixes the ash into the soil. A grass rake is perfect for this task and should lightly turn the first inch of soil. Do not rake a slope if it has a high chance of erosion/topsoil loss.

BROADCASTING If a site has irrigation water, seeding can start immediately. If a site has no water, broadcasting must wait until the second rain. Broadcasting seeds can be done with a seed spreader, granular fertilizer spreader, or by hand. Always place more seed uphill and in areas exposed to wind. Scarecrows, noise makers or reflective ribbons will help deter birds from eating or disturbing the seeds, which is important on slopes without irrigation.

TAPPING Gently tapping the ground after sowing increases germination rates. Tapping pushes the seeds into the ground, enveloping them in moist, nourishing soil. Tapping also prevents the seeds from either being blown away or eaten by predators. Dragging an empty lawn roller or lightly walking over a seeded area is sufficient to set seeds.

If the risk of topsoil loss is high and the area cannot be tapped, then sow the seeds during a light rain. Falling raindrops will help push the seeds into the soil.

MULCH Mulch will not only depower rain and help irrigation percolate but also help protect seeds and prevent them from drying out. The mulch should be thin and light, such as hay, straw, or humus. Heavy and thick mulches can reduce germination rates. Mulching is not necessary if the burned landscape is littered with charred debris.

FERTILIZER Nitrogen, the nutrient most needed by plants, is reduced after a wildfire. However, applying nitrogen fertilizers is rarely recommended. Nitrogen can spur too much growth too quickly. If the seed mix needs nitrogen, like many grasses do, then use a low-nitrogen fertilizer, such as blood meal, and only after the seeds have sprouted. Fertilizers are not recommended in

native and natural landscapes. There is no need to supplement phosphorus and potassium because ash and charred debris supply both.

This slope needs pulse irrigation. Rills at the top of the photo and a buried mow strip at the bottom mean that the slope is getting water faster than it can accept it.

REGULAR IRRIGATION A watering schedule can now begin. Because only the top 4 inches of soil need to be moist, watering must be light and semifrequent. Pulse irrigation is needed on steep slopes to prevent runoff. Pulse irrigation is watering at short durations (about 4 minutes) many times a day. If your slope produces runoff from irrigation, then you need pulse irrigation.

HYDROSEEDING

Hydroseeding, a blend of seed and mulch glued together, has higher germination rates than broadcasting by hand. Sprayed from a truck, hydroseeding is quick and effective but expensive. This type of seeding is used only on slopes with a medium or high risk of topsoil loss. The type of seeds in a hydroseeding mix can be tailored to a specific landscape.

PLANTING: PERENNIALS AND SHRUBS

Planting begins after all the strategies to divert, drain, and depower rainfall and runoff have been employed. Planting is the preferred method of stabilization for slopes with low to medium risk of topsoil loss. Planting on slopes with high risk can increase rates of topsoil loss. High-risk slopes are generally seeded first and planted only after the hill is deemed stable.

PLANT SELECTION

Plant selection affects future risks and costs. The risk of fire and erosion, along with the costs of construction and maintenance, will rise for every degree of incline. All plants should be evaluated methodically based on their ability to meet the following criteria:

The resprouting ability of lemonade berry (*Rhus integrifolia*) and white sage (*Salvia apiana*) helps diffuse the impacts of winter. This picture was taken five months after a wildfire denuded the slope.

- **Proper size:** Larger plants offer more initial erosion control, while smaller plants disrupt and displace less topsoil when planted. As a rule of thumb, use plants in up to 15-gallon containers on low-risk slopes; up to 5-gallon containers on low- to medium-risk slopes; up to 1-gallon containers on medium-risk slopes; and plugs, seeds, and stems of sprouting shrubs on high-risk slopes.

- **Low fuel:** Plant fuels must be kept to a minimum on slopes—hills elongate flames and a 2-foot flame on flat ground grows to 8 feet on a 30% slope. Avoid plants that produce a lot of litter or have twiggy dense interiors, like coyote brush, as well as large reseeding plants and shrubs taller than 18 inches.

- **Ground hugging:** Growth that sprawls on top of the soil helps protects it from the effects of water, wind, and gravity. When shrubs are used as ground covers, choose prostrate and sprawling varieties. Ground-hugging plants also suppress the growth of weeds.

- **Low maintenance:** Because of the difficulties and hazards of working on slopes, select low-maintenance plants. Keeping people and equipment off a slope also helps stabilize it. Consult with your local nursery, Resource Conservation District (RCD), or conservation advocacy organization for the best choices.

- **Low water:** Irrigation supports the health of fire-resistant plants and helps bind the soil together. But too much water promotes weeds and adds unnecessary weight and erosion risk to the slope. Tough plants that need only occasional water are preferred.

- **Resprouting:** If your property has had a wildfire pass through it in the last 100 years, there's a good chance it will happen again. Selecting plants that can rebound from injuries due to cutting, intense heat, or flame contact will help slow topsoil loss following a fire. Some of these plants can produce new growth within weeks after being burned to the ground.

A DEEP-ROOTED CAUTION

Rock is the parent material of most slopes. It becomes topsoil as it fractures and degrades. Deep-rooted plants can speed the fracturing process. They pry apart naturally occurring divisions in the soil and rock, and as these divisions widen, water is able to seep in and create a slick between the two surfaces, increasing the likelihood of small rock and mudslides. Avoid using deep-rooted plants on rocky slopes and instead use shallow-rooted plants that can sprawl across the surface, such as Cape honeysuckle, cranesbill, fleabane, small-leaved ivy, and trailing succulents.

This oak has been prying apart the shale embankment for years, causing unnecessary erosion and work.

Deep-rooted plants are ideal on slopes with several soil horizons or deep topsoil. In these environments, the plants help pin the slope together.

PLANTING POINTERS

- Make sure the plant is watered well the day before planting.

- Measure the root ball before digging your hole, and dig only as deep as the root ball is long.

- Make the hole twice as wide as deep in sandy and silty soils, 1.25 times as wide in dense soils.

- Once the hole is dug, fill with water and allow to drain. Prewetting the soil improves plant health.

- Keep the crown of the plant slightly above the natural grade of the slope.

- Water again after planting.

- Wet and moist soils are prone to

Dig your hole only as deep as the root ball is long and 1.25–2 times as wide, depending on soil type. Berms help direct water toward the new plant.

compaction, so do not tamp the back-filled soil around a plant. Instead, pour the soil around the plant, and let the first few waterings move the soil around the root ball.

- Create berms around the new plant to aid in focused irrigation.

- Delay mulching the surface of new plants until they have overcome transplant shock. You will need to be able to adjust the level of the soil and its moisture.

- Control predators. Young plants are more palatable to some animals and insects, and they may need protection the first year. Methods include wire cages (which can be used to protect roots too); covering with burlap; or using repelling devices, such as scarecrows, reflective ribbon, and noisemakers.

MAINTENANCE FOR EROSION CONTROL

BEFORE THE FIRST BIG STORMS

- Remove debris and vegetation from stormwater-transportation devices, including catch basins, concrete ditches, culverts, curbs, rain gutters, storm streams, and swales.

- Direct sheeting runoff away from bare landscapes.

- Mulch or seed bare soil.

- Remove debris and sediment from behind any device running perpendicular to a slope, such as a check dam or stacked wall.

DURING THE RAIN AND STORMS

- Remove debris and sediment from stormwater-management devices after any rain event of 1 inch or greater.

AS THE RAIN SUBSIDES

- Remove the buildup of debris and sludge from swales and infiltration basins. Give it to garden beds.

- Clean and thin the plants in infiltration basins, microbasins, and swales.

- Seed or plant bare areas.

DURING THE DRY MONTHS

- Audit the irrigation system, looking specifically for any signs of erosion (rills and gullies), overspray (circular stains), or dry-season runoff (algae in curbs).

- Remove bales and fiber rolls before they become a fire hazard.

- Aerate compacted or trampled areas, applying 1–2 inches of fine mulch afterward.

- Repair or replace drain grates and leaf guards.

- Develop a plan for fuel and erosion management.

SUPPORTING YOUR COMMUNITY

CHAPTER 21
COMMUNITY OBLIGATIONS

Whether directly or not, governing bodies have enormous influence on community design and behavior. Maintaining roads and fuel breaks, providing education and code enforcement, managing vegetation and bioutilization projects, and ensuring adequate water supply and pressure will help safeguard the health and safety of the citizens in fire country.

YOUR COMMUNITY NEEDS YOU

Creating a community that can survive a conflagration takes many people and their many different sets of skills. Fire safety is not just about pulling weeds. If you have any of the skills below, please consider volunteering with your local Firewise USA® committee, Fire Safe Council, or any other organization dedicated to community-scale fire protection.

- Bookkeeping

- Community organization: extroversion and passion

- Database management: donor, grantor, and volunteer lists

- Equipment expertise

- Fundraising

- Manual work: mowing, pruning, hauling

- Political advocacy: writing, speaking

- Promotion: artwork, social media, speaking to groups

- Public education: creating brochures, posters, and presentations

- Volunteer management: appreciation, flattery, smiles

Above: Low- to moderate-intensity prescribed burns reduce fuels, reducing the risk of wildfires.

ROADS

The importance of properly designed roads cannot be understated. Surviving an urban conflagration involves both fleeing and fighting, and both demand roads that can allow for two-way traffic and easy navigation during periods of poor visibility. Refer to Chapter 6 ("Roads") for all the details.

COMMUNICATION

Whether inspiring citizens to take action or issuing evacuation orders, the ability of a community to reach its members can make the difference between life and death. Depending on the message to be conveyed, levels of effective communication range greatly, from offering classes and holding community events to posting on social media, sending emergency texts, and making calls. Communication is critical in creating fire-safe communities.

ENFORCEMENT

Compliance with laws for vegetation management is dismally low (see Chapter 1, "Identifying Fire Hazard Areas"). Rates of compliance could grow if fire agencies were more aggressive at enforcing the law. But simply demanding enforcement will not solve a long-standing problem, which is that fire agencies are not designed as enforcement organizations, sometimes lacking both the manpower and the skill for effective enforcement. Furthermore, penalties for noncompliance are civil and equate to fines and liens, which do not impact public property, land tied up in courts (like probate), and absent or ornery property owners. Active enforcement of fire code can help create fire-protected communities, but it is not a silver bullet and will never be able to entirely solve the problem of flammable properties.

VEGETATION MANAGEMENT

Communities manage vast tracts of land—whether in landscapes around public buildings, around roads, or in designated open space—and vegetation management in these areas is essential in creating fire-protected communities. There are three primary ways to manage excess fuels: mechanical clearing, prescribed (controlled) burns, and grazing.

MECHANICAL CLEARING

Mechanical clearing includes chopping, cutting, digging, mowing, pulling, scraping, and tilling the fuels to reduce the risk. Mechanical clearing is the most common method of vegetation management. (Prescribed burns may not be practically or politically feasible, and grazing requires just the right type of vegetation, topography, and personnel.)

PRESCRIBED BURNS

Prescribed means that burning will occur only in ideal conditions, based on a formula of temperature, humidity, wind speed, topography, and type of fuel. In fire-adapted landscapes, prescribed burns provide many benefits. They reduce fuels by as much as 50% and can reduce the risk of fire by 90%. They are low- to moderate-intensity fires that allow more than 80% of the trees to survive. They favor native plants and animals. They leave roots intact and debris littered across a landscape, which reduces topsoil loss. They produce fewer air pollutants, both gaseous and particulate, than a wildfire burning the same area. They are less expensive when compared to mowing, sometimes by as much as 5 times, and they are at least 10 times less expensive that battling a wildfire.

GRAZING

Cattle, goats, sheep, and even llamas have been called up to clear land throughout the nation. Properly managed grazing can increase not only wildflowers, perennials, and grasses but also a variety of pollinators, birds, and small animals. Grazing can also be used to restore fertility to landscapes in a state of deterioration. However, overgrazing is damaging and can lead to erosion, tainted water bodies, and a decrease in a landscape's productivity and diversity. Out-of-season

Managed herds of grazers have been employed to protect communities for centuries. They can dramatically reduce the abundance of flash fuels.

grazing can reduce the amount of seeds in the soil and undermine ecological processes, such as the nesting of birds and foraging by pollinators.

Scale typically determines the use of grazers. Land managers with less than 5 acres may find mowing less expensive, whereas a city managing thousands of acres may discover that grazers are cheaper. The person employed to oversee grazing must understand the principles of seasonal and rotational grazing and the signs of overgrazing. Goats are the most common grazer because they eat scrub and shrub (not grass) and can reach difficult terrain. Sheep eat grass.

BIOUTILIZATION

A community committed to fire protection and vegetation management must be equally committed to handling large amounts of greenwaste. When inexpensive and readily available avenues for greenwaste are not available, costs to remove vegetative fuels increase, decreasing likelihood of removal. Of all the current avenues for greenwaste, which include burning, composting, creating product, direct and indirect energy generation, and landfilling, the most promising are creating product and direct and indirect energy generation.

No matter the strategy for greenwaste, anticipating and supporting the increase is critical to sustaining fire-protected communities.

Municipalities and agencies managing large volumes of greenwaste are in a much better position than single-property owners or small neighborhoods to repurpose vegetative material. These organizations have economies of scale and existing infrastructure that can reduce the costs of reuse.

Biochar, used as a soil amendment, is one of the products that can be made from greenwaste.

Some of the things greenwaste can be turned into include the following:

1. Mulch and compost

2. Renewable energy

- Compost heat. Water pipes running through large piles of compost can be used to heat small structures and small greenhouses.

- Electricity, either from incineration, where the greenwaste is dried, chipped, and/or pressed into material for combustion, or from the biogas (methane) produced from the decomposition of material within a landfill. Many modern landfills are designed to capture and use the methane they produce.

- Ethanol. Although more energy intensive and expensive, some types of waste can be made into ethanol.

3. Product

- Boutique lumber. It is favored by many fine carpenters, green-build architects, and hobbyists. The marginal logs and big branches can be turned into benches, borders, fence posts, pallets, planks, railings, and retaining walls.

ADEQUATE WATER PRESSURE AND SUPPLY

Earthquakes, lightning, and wildfires can knock out the electricity, creating a huge problem if the distribution of water is dependent on transmitted electricity. The problem is compounded if the supply of water comes from one centralized source. Wise communities invest in many gravity-fed water-storage systems. Smart communities decentralize water storage and pumping capacity, which means that water-storage facilities, such as aquifers, lakes, and tanks, have their own energy, energy storage, and water pumps.

POLLUTION

Whether air, water, heat, light, or noise, pollution from urbanized areas dramatically affects landscapes and natural processes. Air and water are the two most pervasive types pertaining to urban wildfires.

AIR POLLUTION

Air pollution affects plants, but not all impacts are harmful. Particulate pollution is particularly bad for plants because it coats the leaves, lowering photosynthesis and productivity, decreasing resilience to droughts, and increasing likelihood of pest infestation and disease. On the other hand, gaseous pollution benefits some plants by acidifying and nitrifying the soil. So vegetation subject to urban pollution grows faster, but dies sooner, than vegetation in wild areas. While ground-level ozone, a latent pollutant of burning fossil fuels, is generally bad for plants, not all react the same way. Birch, pine, and sycamore are more easily injured than maple and oak.

WATER POLLUTION

The fertilizers, pesticides, and water we give our landscapes do not always stay on the property. They commonly flow off as dry-season runoff and degrade natural storm-drain systems or soak into the ground and either pollute groundwater or seep back to the surface. The pollutants that seep to the surface increase the growth of invasive plants.

GROUNDWATER

Many communities and industries rely on groundwater to meet their needs. This can—and has—lowered the water table, as does channeling water out of streams for urban use. When the water table is lowered, the plant communities that depend on being able to reach it die. This phenomenon is visible along the nation's foothills and watershed corridors. While droughts get the bulk of the blame for our nation's dry conditions, retreating groundwater supplies also contribute greatly.

CHAPTER 22
MANAGING FIRE COUNTRY'S THREE TYPES OF LANDSCAPES

The model described here was created 20 years ago as a way to approach landscape care and education efforts. I have used and refined it ever since. It helps make complex ideas digestible. However, dividing all the nation's fire-prone landscapes into three broad categories is problematic: generalization, misclassification, and overrepresentation are likely.

Despite the drawbacks, this model helps cultivate beneficial land-management practices. How homeowners maintain their properties is much different than how state parks do—and rightly so; what is beneficial for one could be damaging for another. Management practices vary as wildly as the landscape itself. To communicate these differences, the message must be as nimble as it is simple.

Above: The landscapes within fire-prone communities can be categorized as one of three types: native, natural, or domestic. These descriptions define boundaries, identifying areas that *can* burn, *will* burn, and should absolutely *never* burn. **Top:** The structure in this picture is on its own. This is a native landscape, and environmental forces rule.

A native landscape is one that continues to be defined by environmental forces, such as large predators, floods, infestation, storms, and wildfires.

THE NATIVE LANDSCAPE

DESCRIPTION

The native landscape is one whose character continues to be developed by environmental forces, such as apex predators, floods, infestations, storms, and wildfires. Humans play an indirect role in influencing this type of landscape, and it is virtually undeveloped.

All the wonder and horror of ecological processes are encouraged in native landscapes—bears and lions are allowed to roam, mosquitoes and wasps are allowed to menace, and fires and floods are allowed to meander for weeks, if not months. The needs of the fauna and flora outweigh those of humans in this landscape.

WHERE FOUND

A native landscape is generally no less than 250 acres, and even that is considered small. At this scale, natural processes such as those mentioned above can roam without severely threatening human inhabitants. National and state parks, abandoned agriculture and grazing land, retired military sites, sparsely inhabited islands, and coastal marshes can be designated, created, or managed as native landscapes.

UNIQUE ASPECTS OF MANAGEMENT

Native ecosystems have had tens of thousands of years to evolve to fires, floods, freezes, droughts, and even massive infestations. The more naturally and historically disturbed a site was, the greater the degree of specialization in the native species. When any of these disruptive forces are removed from a landscape, the advantage of the specialty is diminished and the species become less competitive.

A wildfire, for example, greatly alters a landscape and favors the adapted species. Fire devours nitrogen in the soil, it leaves potassium-rich ash, and its heat and acidic smoke entice many native cones and seeds to sprout. Wildfires also kill many types of animals, insects, and plants. Fire-adapted ecosystems rely on the low nitrogen, heat scarification, and lack of competitors and predators.

To effectively maintain the health of a native landscape, the conditions that influenced its development must be restored. This may require isolating the landscape from urban influences and letting these events naturally occur. Encouraging the landscape's natural cycles will promote indigenous plants and animals, help reduce aggressive exotic plants, and help keep plant fuels from building to conflagration levels. Letting wildfires go and employing controlled burns are sensible land-management practices in native landscapes.

HOW TO DEFEND A STRUCTURE

Structures built in native landscapes need to be designed and maintained so that a fire can burn around them. Typically, these structures are isolated from community resources and must have the capacity to independently defend themselves. Nonflammable building materials and severe vegetation clearance around the structures are musts.

THE NATURAL LANDSCAPE

DESCRIPTION

A natural landscape is one where human concerns outweigh those of the fauna and flora but environmental forces still play a large role in determining its character. The plants are anything that can survive and reproduce. Humans do not actively control the nature of the landscape, but will rush in anytime it poses a threat—wildfires are quickly extinguished, flooding is channelized, eroding hills are seeded, and aggressive animals are culled.

This type of landscape is a hybrid, because it exists along with humans and has a combination of native and nonnative naturalized plants. The plants and animals found in these areas are not as specialized as those in the native landscape and can adapt to a wide range of conditions. Animals include deer, possums, raccoons, skunks, and turkeys. This landscape is highly fire suppressed.

The natural landscape is greatly affected by human development. The impacts of pollution (air, light, noise, and water), increased heat, and recreational use of the land profoundly alter ecological processes. Invasive species are common in natural landscapes because of all these factors.

WHERE FOUND

Natural landscapes can be any size and will commonly blend into a native landscape. They can be found between houses, on vacated properties, or on the outskirts of ranchland. They can be nature parks, small biological reserves, or unused municipal easements. No matter their location or size, natural landscapes are always found around urbanized areas; these are the landscapes where we do not want natural forces to rule but our reach does not dictate otherwise.

UNIQUE ASPECTS OF MANAGEMENT

Flammable plant fuels must be kept low in natural landscapes because of their proximity to people, property, and infrastructure. Reducing excess plant fuels requires either prescribed burns, mechanical clearing, or grazing. Prescribed burns can take place under trees and on small lots and are a relatively inexpensive way to clear large areas. However, getting public support is difficult. Manually clearing is easier to sell the public on, but it typically costs more, favors nonnative plants and animals, and on steep slopes can cause more erosion than burning does. Both approaches require consistency and community involvement.

Managing natural landscapes can be difficult. Sometimes landowners are absent or apathetic. Sometimes an agency or community lacks the funds for massive renewal projects. And sometimes, a community may have the money, but public debate keeps anything from happening. One thing is for sure,

Natural landscapes are found as easily in the wildlands as they are in urban areas. These types of landscapes have the implicit goal of protecting humans but rarely receive our attention.

though—the safety of the communities that border the landscape outweighs all other goals. If excess fuels are not removed, a wildfire will eventually engulf the landscape and endanger everything surrounding it.

It's hard to see the homes in this picture because of the dense tree cover, but they are there. This valley is mostly a natural landscape and contains large private residences, many community easements (trail systems), and public parks maintained to mimic native landscapes. The residents have planted very little of the plant material, and the trees include native fir, madrone, and oak intermixed with naturalized acacia, cypress, and eucalyptus. The density, plant type, and age of this landscape make it a dangerous and combustible valley in which to live.

Community participation and individual responsibility must replace fire as the dominant force in natural landscapes. Strong public education programs are needed to overcome the negative opinions of massive vegetation management (burning or manual clearing).

HOW TO DEFEND A STRUCTURE

At the very least, a natural landscape should help slow a fire. People managing natural landscapes must maintain high accessibility and safety. Service and fire roads must be kept clear. Neighborhood pathways must be clearly marked and maintained. Diseased and dead vegetation must be continually removed. And every three to eight years trees and large shrubs must be thinned. It is not an understatement to say that much of this book was written for the people living in natural landscapes.

THE DOMESTIC LANDSCAPE/ A FIRESCAPED GARDEN

DESCRIPTION

A domestic landscape is designed and maintained. Environmental influences such as fire, floods, and climatic extremes should have the least impact on these landscapes. A domestic landscape exists because of humans, and in most cases it is dependent on humans.

WHERE FOUND

Domestic landscapes are those that surround structures. They are meant for human use and are typically dependent on humans for their health. Residences and commercial spaces, golf courses and botanic gardens, regional parks and nature centers are all domestic landscapes because without continual care they would evolve to weedy natural landscapes.

Interestingly, the types of plants in a landscape do not determine whether it is domestic. There are many native-plant botanic gardens that are domestic because without constant human intervention, they would be overrun by unwanted plants.

UNIQUE ASPECTS OF MANAGEMENT

It is in domestic landscapes where the law carries the greatest weight. A wildfire must be stopped in domestic landscapes; natural landscapes must slow it. In fire hazard areas, all property owners—residential, commercial, and public—are legally required to maintain defensible space around their structures. The amount of defensible space required varies among regions but is generally 30–100 feet.

HOW TO DEFEND A STRUCTURE

In fire-prone areas, a domestic landscape should possess at least one of two characteristics: it must either be able to defend itself from a wildfire or be a welcoming beacon to firefighters so they can defend it. Either approach demands firescaping. A domestic landscape that is not maintained will become a natural landscape and can no longer stop a wildfire. A land manager's energy, creativity, and diligence replaces fire and creates protection. Luckily, helping the land manager maintain domestic and natural landscapes is the purpose of this book.

With a delightful mix of flowering vines, succulents, and native plants, this domestic landscape does a fantastic job of protecting the residence. Without continual care, annual grasses and flammable scrub plants would overrun it.

FURTHER INFORMATION

GLOSSARY

BIOUTILIZATION Making use of greenwaste for such purposes as energy generation, mulch, and products.

CHECK DAMS Devices constructed in a gully or swale to slow flowing water or catch debris. The dams can be small, like rock, or large, like chain-link fencing.

COMBUSTIBILITY A term used to describe the amount of heat a plant or landscape produces when it is on fire. Combustibility is related to moisture content, density, and chemical composition.

CONFLAGRATION A large, uncontrolled, and destructive fire. Usually associated with strong winds that carry firebrands over natural and man-made firebreaks.

CONTROLLED BURN Burning piles of debris, typically vegetation. In most residential areas, these fires require a permit.

CROWN Can apply to both the top and the bottom of a plant. The entire branch structure of a plant is its top crown (*canopy* is another word for it). The sometimes bulbous union where the roots meet the top structure is called the root crown.

DEFENSIBLE SPACE A legal classification in fire hazard areas and a zone around a structure that must remain fire resistant. The legal requirements range from 30 feet to 200 feet. The first 30 feet are the most important and must have low fuels, discontinuity of fuels, and moderate to high levels of plant moisture.

DOMESTIC LANDSCAPE A landscape that is planned and regularly maintained. Home gardens and city parks are examples of domestic landscapes.

DORMANCY The annual slowing of a plant's metabolism. Dormancy is an adaptation to reoccurring environmental pressures, such as drought or freezes.

DRY WALLS Stacked rock walls used to channel, direct, or slow sheeting water. They are common at the toe of slopes.

EMERGENCY WATER Water accessible during an emergency. Property owners can manage their own emergency water systems using a large source, such as a cistern or pool; pumps; and hoses. These systems are used to prewet a property or fight a fire.

EROSION The separation and transportation of soil particles by water, wind, gravity, and activity. Includes debris flows, landslides, soil slips, and topsoil loss.

FIBER ROLL Straw, rice, and coconut waste that have been processed and bound to create long rolls. Laid out across the face of a slope, fiber rolls are used to reduce topsoil loss. They must be partially buried and staked.

FILTER FABRIC Commonly used on construction sites, filter fabric has a variety of uses. It can be used to protect storm drains from sedimentation; as a layer to separate soil from inorganic mulches; and even as a windscreen to help remove dust. There are many types of filter fabrics.

FIRE ADAPTED Plants that have evolved to survive reoccurring wildfires. Many have developed adaptations that help them reproduce following a fire, including resin-protected and fire-stimulated seeds and cones; accelerated maturity; resprouting and nitrogen-fixing abilities; thick seed coats; and, as in the case of redwoods, thick bark and copious amounts of litter (ensuring a fire and their survival in it).

FIREBRAND A windblown ember.

FIREBREAK An area that contains little or no ignitable fuels. A firebreak can be a freeway, road, parking lot, driveway, walkway, or concrete patio. Firefighters typically stage a defense in a firebreak.

FIRE DEPENDENT A plant or ecosystem that requires fire either to aid in its reproduction or to maintain its stability. California's coastal scrub community, for example, is said to be fire dependent.

FIRE LADDER Any plant or grouping of plants that would allow a ground fire to climb into a tree.

FIRE HAZARD AREA Any place likely to be overrun or greatly influenced by a wildfire. These areas are divided into three classes: moderate, high, or very high. These classifications are made by evaluating an area's proximity to wildlands, the likelihood of the wildlands drying, the chance of fire weather, the type of terrain, the type and condition of the plants, the ability to mobilize evacuation and emergency responses, and the area's prior history with wildfire.

FIRE PATHWAY A grouping of plants that allows a fire to travel across a property.

FIRE PRONE A plant or plant community that has a long and documented history of igniting and sustaining fires. The coastal sage scrub community is considered fire prone and has many fire-prone plants. See also *pyrophyte.*

FIRE RESISTANT A plant or material that has the ability to resist the effects of fire. A fire-resistant plant might ignite but is less likely to than others and does not sustain a flame for long. It will also resprout after a fire. These plants are recommended for Zones 2 and 3.

FIRE RETARDANT A plant or material that will actively retard a fire. Fire-retardant plants have low fuels and high moisture, which means they are more likely to sizzle and wilt than produce a flame. Succulents, hostas, and yarrow are some of the many fire-retardant plants. These plants are recommended for Zones 1 and 2.

FIRESCAPING A style of property management that aims to ensure the safety of a property's occupants and structures.

FIRE SUPPRESSED A politically debated term commonly used to describe a landscape that has adapted to the reoccurrence of fire by becoming overgrown, so that when fires are extinguished, they leave huge fuel loads and extreme fire danger for surrounding areas. Fire suppression can have other negative consequences, such as enabling diseases, fungi, insects, and weeds.

FIRE WEATHER A combination of low humidity, high temperatures, and winds. Fire weather becomes lethal when the moisture in plants drops to ignition levels.

FLAMMABILITY The fire potential of a plant, house, or landscape. The fire potential of an object is based on its combustibility, ignitability, and sustainability.

FLASH FUEL Any object that is relatively easy to ignite. Natural grasses, particularly annual varieties, are considered flash fuels. Canvas awnings and stacks of newspapers are also examples of flash fuels.

FOEHN WINDS These winds are exceptionally dangerous and are distinguished by a rapid rise in temperature and a big drop in humidity. They are often fast, gusty, and erratic. Foehn winds occur throughout the world and many parts of the United States. They are also called Chinook, devil, diablo, katabolic, Santa Ana, and sundowner winds.

FUEL BREAK An area with low amounts of ignitable fuel. See also *greenbelt*.

GARDEN ZONE The first 30 feet from a structure. The garden zone must be designed and maintained to withstand an aggressive assault of firebrands and intense heat. It is also the area where firefighters will work. See also *Zone 1*.

GPM Gallons per minute. Describes the rate of water flow. Important when designing an emergency watering system.

GRAZER An animal that reduces fuels by eating vegetation. Goats are the most common because they eat broad-leaved plants, known as scrub in fire country. Sheep, llamas, and cows generally eat grass and grain.

GREENBELT An area low in ignitable fuels. The primary goal of a greenbelt is to stop a ground fire. See also *Zone 2*.

GULLIES AND RILLS Areas of concentrated runoff that cause erosion and indented paths. Rills are small gullies.

HIGH-PRESSURE WATERING SYSTEM A watering system that requires high pressure to irrigate a large area. Devices used include impulse and pop-up sprinkler heads, and garden and firefighting hoses.

IGNITABILITY The temperatures and conditions required to cause a plant or object to burst into flames. The ignitability of plants is determined by moisture content, leaf size, and chemical composition.

LANDSLIDES A mass of sliding rocks, soil, or mud.

LIMB UP To remove the lower branches of a shrub or tree. The goal of limbing up is to prevent a ground fire from climbing into a tree. Limbing up young plants is ill-advised; it reduces the girth of the trunk when increasing its length, creating a plant more prone to wind breakage.

LOW-PRESSURE WATERING SYSTEM A watering system that requires low pressure to irrigate precise locations in exact amounts. Devices used include inline drip emitters, microsprinklers, misters, and soaker tubing.

MATTING A device laid over the top of a slope to slow runoff and reduce topsoil loss. Examples include jute mesh, lattice, and chain-link fencing.

NATIVE LANDSCAPE A landscape where environmental forces such as fires, floods, and apex predators continue to roam and shape its character. Human development is almost nonexistent in these areas.

NATURAL LANDSCAPE A landscape where apex predators, fires, and floods are eradicated because of the risk to urban interests and infrastructure. Unfortunately, there is little other maintenance. These landscapes are fire suppressed and overgrown. Residential development in native landscapes creates natural landscapes, which consist of both native and exotic species.

OVERHANG Any part of a structure that juts out over a slope. Overhangs are supported by stilts, expose their underbelly, and are common on sloped properties.

PERCENTAGE OF SLOPE The rise of an incline divided by its run then multiplied by 100.

PRESCRIBED BURN A method of fuel reduction and habitat restoration. Used in native and natural landscapes, prescribed fires can be started only with community support and can be ignited only with a prescription, which is a matrix of the ideal temperature, humidity, fuel moisture, and wind behavior.

PYROPHYTE A plant that is easy to ignite. These plants generally have high oil content, twiggy growth, a lot of deadwood, and/or a short life span. Cedar, cypress, and juniper are considered pyrophytic. See also *fire prone*.

RILLS AND GULLIES Areas of concentrated runoff that cause erosion and indented paths. Rills are small gullies.

RIPRAP Large pieces of rock or broken concrete used to line swales, make check dams, or cover a vulnerable slope.

RUNOFF Water that runs over a surface. Runoff occurs in soils that are receiving water faster than they can absorb it, eventually creating rills and enlarging gullies.

SEDIMENTATION The deposit of suspended particles of soil or rock by water or wind. Occurs when the water or wind slows to the point that the weight of the particle is greater than the carrying force of the water or wind.

SIGHT LINES The ability to see down a road. For traffic moving at 25 mph, 155 feet of forward visibility is considered safe.

SKIRT A barrier that prevents heat, firebrands, and fires from getting under an overhang. Skirts run from the bottom of an overhang to the ground and are made from metal sheets or fire-resistant plywood.

SOIL SLIP Small, sliding movements of rocks, soil, or mud.

SPARK ARRESTER A noncombustible, corrosion-resistant mesh that covers the outlets of chimneys, stovepipes, and landscape equipment such as chippers and chainsaws. These simple devices reduce chances of ignition by catching sparks.

SUSTAINABILITY A plant or landscape's ability to keep a fire going. Sustainability is determined by the amount of dry fuel a plant or landscape has.

SWALE A drainage device that is typically cut into the land and used to channel and transport water. Swales should not exceed a 4% grade and can be vegetated, lined with rock, or protected with concrete.

TOPSOIL The top layer of soil. This typically rich soil can be 1 inch deep or less on southwest-facing slopes and 1 foot deep or greater in northeast-facing canyons. Topsoil has more nutrients, better structure, and quicker water absorption than subsoils.

TRANSITION ZONE Generally starting 70 feet from a structure and extending to the end of the defensible space, this zone separates a domestic landscape from a natural or native one. The goal of the transition zone is to dramatically slow a fire. See also *Zone 3*.

UNDERSTORY The environment under a canopy of trees.

WILDFIRE An uncontrolled fire.

WILLOW WATTLE A tightly wrapped bundle of willow twigs. Partially buried and staked, these rolls will sprout if watered and are used to reduce erosion, protect the banks of streams, and aid in ecological restoration.

ZONE 1 The area immediately around a structure. This zone should be able to endure firebrands and intense heat without igniting. See also *garden zone*.

ZONE 2 The area just outside the garden zone. This zone must be capable of stopping a wildfire. See also *greenbelt*.

ZONE 3 The area just outside the greenbelt. This zone must be able to dramatically slow a fire. See also *transition zone*.

REFERENCES AND FURTHER READING

INTRODUCTION: CHAPTERS 1–4

California Building Code, Chapter 7A(SFM): "Materials and Construction Methods for Exterior Wildfire Exposure."

Cal Fire (California Department of Forestry and Fire Protection). 2012. "California's Wildland-Urban Interface Code Information." Accessed August 24, 2018. fire.ca.gov/fire_prevention/fire_prevention_wildland_codes.

Cheney, Phil, and Andrew Sullivan. *Grassfires: Fuel, Weather and Fire Behaviour.* CRIRO Publishing: Australia, 1997.

Chong, Jia-Rui, and Doug Smith. "Some Homes Had Shields to Ward Off Wildfires." *Los Angeles Times,* April 1, 2004.

Crosby, Bill. "Our Wild Fire: History Shows That Nearly All of California Is Designed to Burn." *Sunset,* June 1992. Reprint.

Dana Jr., Richard Henry. *Two Years Before the Mast.* Thomas Groom & Co., 1851.

Ferguson, Gary. *Land on Fire: The New Reality of Wildfire in the West.* Portland, OR: Timber Press, 2017.

Fish, Peter. "Chaparral." *Sunset,* April 1994.

Home Landscaping Guide for Lake Tahoe and Vicinity. University of Nevada Cooperative Extension, 1999.

Kent, Douglas. *Firescaping: Creating Fire-Resistant Landscapes, Gardens, and Properties in California's Diverse Environments.* Birmingham, AL: Wilderness Press, 2005.

Michaels, Patrick, and Eric Sagara. "Should Development Be Extinguished on California's Fire-Prone Hills?" The Center for Investigative Reporting. *Reveal,* July 3, 2018.

Moore, Howard E. *Protecting Residences From Wildfires: A Guide for Homeowners, Lawmakers, and Planners.* Berkeley, CA: USDA Pacific Southwest Forest and Range Experiment Station, 1981.

Morrison, Peter H., and George Wooten. "Analysis and Comments on the Yarnell Hill Fire in Arizona and the Current Fire Situation in the United States." Pacific Biodiversity Institute. July 2013. At pacificbio.org/initiatives/fire/yarnell_fire.html.

National Fire Protection Association. *n.d.* "Top Causes of Fire." Accessed April 22, 2019. nfpa.org/public-education/by-topic/top-causes-of-fire.

"Protecting Your Home Against Brushfire." *Sunset,* September 1983 and September 1985. Reprint.

Radtke, Klaus W. H. *Living More Safely in the Chaparral-Urban Interface.* Berkeley, CA: USDA Pacific Southwest Forest and Range Experiment Station, June 1983.

FIRESCAPING: CHAPTERS 5–15

Barkley, Yvonne C., Chris Schnepf, and Jack Cohen. "Protecting and Landscaping Homes in the Wildland/Urban Interface." Idaho Forest, Wildlife, and Range Experiment Station Bulletin No. 67. University of Idaho Extension. USDA Forest Service Rocky Mountain Research Station, 2005.

Cal Fire (California Department of Forestry and Fire Protection). 2018. "Fire Prevention." Accessed August 19, 2018. calfire.ca.gov/fire_prevention/fire_prevention.

---. 2018. "Prepare for a Wildfire: Hardening Your Home." Accessed August 22, 2018. readyforwildfire.org/hardening-your-home.

Calflora. calflora.org.

California Department of Forestry. 2000. *Fire Safety Guides for Residential Development in California.*

City of Grants Pass, OR. *n.d.* "Fire-Resistant vs. Highly Flammable Plants." Accessed August 20, 2018. grantspassoregon.gov/289/fire-resistant-vs-highly-flammable-plant.

Dines, Nicholas, and Kyle Brown. *Landscape Architect's Portable Handbook.* New York: McGraw-Hill, 2001.

Federal Emergency Management Agency. September 2008. "Eaves, Overhangs, and Soffits: Home Builder's Guide to Construction in Wildfire Zones." Technical Fact Sheet No. 6. Accessed August 19, 2018. fema.gov/media-library-data/20130726-1652-20490-2869/fema_p_737_fs_6.pdf.

Home Landscaping Guide for Lake Tahoe and Vicinity. Reno, NV: University of Nevada Cooperative Extension, 2001.

Hopper, Leonard J. *Landscape Architectural Graphic Standards.* Hoboken, NJ: John Wiley & Sons, 2007.

International Urban-Wildland Interface Code. 2003. International Code Council Inc.

National Fire Protection Association. *n.d.* "Firewise USA." Accessed January 13, 2019. nfpa.org/public-education/by-topic/wildfire/firewise-usa.

Hopper, Leonard J. *Landscape Architectural Graphic Standards.* Hoboken, NJ: John Wiley & Sons, 2007.

Institute for Business and Home Safety. 2001. "Is Your Home Protected from Wildfire Disaster? A Homeowner's Guide to Wildfire Retrofit." Accessed August 19, 2018. ohp.parks.ca.gov/pages/1054/files/wildfireretrofit_ibhs.pdf.

International Urban-Wildland Interface Code. 2003. International Code Council Inc.

Lady Bird Johnson Wildflower Center. Native Plant Database. wildflower.org/plants.

Las Pilitas Nursery. laspilitas.com.

Ludwig, Art. *Water Storage: Tanks, Cisterns, Aquifers, and Ponds for Domestic Supply, Fire and Emergency Use,* 2nd ed. Santa Barbara, CA: Oasis Design, 2009.

Maire, Richard G. *Landscape for Fire Protection.* University of California, Agricultural Extension Service, 1969.

Mercker, David, Carol Reese, and Wayne K. Clatterbuck. *n.d.* "Landscaping Guidelines to Protect Your Home from Wildfire." Publication SP685. Tennessee Department of Agriculture Division of Forestry.

Missouri Botanical Garden. Plant Finder. missouribotanicalgarden.org/plantfinder/plantfindersearch.aspx.

Montgomery, Kenneth R., and P. C. Cheo. *Fire-Retardant Plants for Brush Fire Prevention in Hillside Residential Areas.* Research Division, Los Angeles State and County Arboretum. *Lasca Leaves,* September 1970.

Montgomery, Kenneth R., and P. C. Cheo. "Moisture and Salt Effects on Fire Retardance in Plants." Research Division, Los Angeles State and County Arboretum. *American Journal of Botany* 56, no. 9 (October 1969): 1028–1032.

National Fire Protection Association. Public Education. Accessed August 15, 2018. nfpa.org/public-education.

Northern California Chapter of the American Society of Landscape Architects: Fire Recovery Task Force. *n.d.* "Landscape Considerations to Reduce Fire Danger."

Perry, Bob. *Trees and Shrubs for Dry California Landscapes.* Claremont, CA: Land Design Publishing, 1987.

The Sunset Western Garden Book. Menlo Park, CA: Lane Publishing Co., 1990–2018.

University of California Division of Agriculture and Natural Resources. 1994. *Pests of Landscape Tree and Shrubs: An Integrated Pest Management Guide.* Publication 3359.

---. 2007. *Home Landscaping for Fire.* Publication 8228.

---. 2018. "Homeowner's Wildfire Mitigation Guide." Accessed August 20, 2018. ucanr.edu/sites/wildfire.

University of Nevada Cooperative Extension. 2001. *Home Landscaping Guide for Lake Tahoe and Vicinity.*

MAINTENANCE: CHAPTERS 16–18

Bossard, Carla C., John M. Randelland, and Marc C. Husbovsky. *Invasive Plants of California's Wildlands.* Berkeley, CA: University of California Press, 2000.

Falk, Donald A., Margaret A. Palmer, and Joy B. Zedler, eds. *Foundations of Restoration Ecology.* Washington, DC: Island Press, 2006.

Farnham, Delbert S. *A Property Owner's Guide to Reducing the Wildfire Threat.* Jackson, CA: University of California Cooperative Extension, Amador County, 1992.

Finstad, Kristin, Christiane Parry, and Eben Schwartz. *Digging In: A Guide to Community-Based Habitat Restoration.* San Francisco, CA: California Coastal Commission, 2008.

Holloran, Pete, Anouk Mackenzie, Sharon Farrell, and Doug Johnson. *The Weed Workers' Handbook: A Guide to Removing Bay Area Invasive Plants.* Berkeley, CA: The Watershed Project and California Invasive Plant Council, 2004.

Juhren, M. C., and Kenneth R. Montgomery. "Long-Term Responses of Cistus and Certain Other Introduced Shrubs on Disturbed Wildland Sites in Southern California." *Ecology* 58, no.1 (Winter 1977).

Kent, Douglas. *California Friendly: A Maintenance Guide for Landscapers, Gardeners and Land Managers.* Orange, CA: Douglas Kent + Associates, 2017.

Libby, W. J., and K. A. Rodrigues. "Revegetating the 1991 Oakland–Berkeley Hills Burn." *Fremontia* 20, no. 1 (January 1992): 12–18.

Mann, Charles C. *1491: New Revelations of the Americas Before Columbus.* New York: Vintage Press, 2006.

Peck, Sheila. *Planning for Biodiversity.* Washington, DC: Island Press, 1998.

Perrow, Martin R., and Anthony J. Davy, eds. *Handbook of Ecological Restoration: Volume 2, Restoration in Practice.* Cambridge, England: Cambridge University Press, 2002.

Smaus, Robert. *52 Weeks in the California Garden.* Los Angeles: Los Angeles Times Syndicate Books, 1996.

The Sunset Western Garden Book. Menlo Park, CA: Lane Publishing Co., 1990–2018.

Svihra, Pavel. "The Oakland–Berkeley Hills Fire: Lessons for the Arborist." *Journal of Arboriculture* 18, no. 5 (September 1992).

Weed Management Handbook. Pacific Northwest Pest Management Handbooks. Updated annually by Pacific Northwest Land Grant Universities and available online at pnwpest.org/pnw/weeds.

Yang, Sarah. "Let It Burn: Prescribed Fires Pose Little Danger to Forest Ecology." University of California Berkeley News Center. June 11, 2012.

POSTFIRE RECOVERY: CHAPTERS 19 AND 20

Hillside Landscaping. Menlo Park, CA: Sunset Publishing Corporation, 2002.

Hopper, Leonard J. *Landscape Architectural Graphic Standards.* Hoboken, NJ: John Wiley & Sons, 2007.

Kent, Douglas. *Ocean Friendly Gardens: A How-To Gardening Guide to Help Restore a Healthy Coast and Ocean.* San Clemente, CA: Surfrider Foundation, 2009.

Libby, W. J., and K. A. Rodrigues. "Revegetating the 1991 Oakland–Berkeley Hills Burn." *Fremontia* 20, no. 1 (January 1992): 12–18.

Radtke, Klaus W. H. *Living More Safely in the Chaparral-Urban Interface.* Berkeley, CA: USDA Pacific Southwest Forest and Range Experiment Station, June 1983.

Strom, Steven, and Kurt Nathan. *Site Engineering for Landscape Architects,* 3rd ed. Hoboken, NJ: John Wiley & Sons, 1998.

USDA Soil Conservation Service (now the Natural Resources Conservation Services). 1930–present. "The Universal Soil Loss Equation (USLE)."

COMMUNITY OBLIGATIONS: CHAPTERS 21 AND 22

Biswell, Harold H. *Prescribed Burning in California Wildlands Vegetation Management.* Berkeley, CA: University of California Press, 1989.

Ferguson, Gary. *Land on Fire: The New Reality of Wildfire in the West.* Portland, OR: Timber Press, 2017.

Hopper, Leonard J. *Landscape Architectural Graphic Standards.* Hoboken, NJ: John Wiley & Sons, 2007.

Morrison, Peter H., and George Wooten. *Analysis and Comments on the Yarnell Hill Fire in Arizona and the Current Fire Situation in the United States.* Winthrop, WA: Pacific Biodiversity Institute, July 2013. Accessed August 19, 2018. pacificbio.org/initiatives/fire/yarnell_fire.html.

National Fire Protection Association. "Firewise USA." Accessed January 13, 2019. nfpa.org/public-education/by-topic/wildfire/firewise-usa.

Yang, Sarah. "Let It Burn: Prescribed Fires Pose Little Danger to Forest Ecology." University of California Berkeley News Center. June 11, 2012.

INDEX

A
attracting emergency personnel, 38–39

B
bioutilization, 132–133
breathing easier in wildfires, 19–22
building codes, identifying fire hazard areas, 5
burning debris, 16

C
checklists
    design. *See design checklists*
    road maintenance, 32–33
climate change, 2
climatic extremes, 7
community obligations, 130–133
costs
    of firefighting, 3
    of fire protection, 13–14

D
debris flows following fires, reducing, 27
defensible space, 12, 25, 43–45, 85
design checklists
    driveways, 40–41
    ridgetops, 55–56
    roads, 30–32
    slopes, 50
    small properties, 53–54
    structures, 35–39
    understory, 57
driveway safety, design checklist, 40–41
drought, 7

E
ecological costs of fires, 3
emergency
    access, 93
    attracting personnel, 38–39
    response and terrain, 10
    supply kits, 18–19
    watering systems, 86–90
erosion
    control on slopes, 52
    control after wildfire, 111–128
    following urban wildfires, 3
evacuation, 12, 18–25

F
fences, 81–83
fire codes, compliance barriers, 13–14
fire hazard areas, identifying, defining, 4–10
fire hydrants, 32
fire protection
    and equipment use, burning debris, 16–17
    expenses of, 13–14
    during a fire, 18–22
    and ignition areas, 17
fire weather awareness, 15
firefighting costs, 3
fires
    ecological costs of, 3
    global causes of, 2
    nature of, 4–5
foehn winds, 6–7
freezes, 7
fuel break/greenbelt (zone 2), 45–47
fuel tanks, 46

G
garden paths, 81
garden zone/defensible space (zone 1), 43–45
gardens, firescaped, 137–138
grazing, 131–132
greenbelt/fuel break (zone 2), 45–47
greenbelts, amount required, 50–51
groundwater, 133–134

H
hedges, 85, 103–104
homes
    protecting inside, during fires, 20
    protecting outside, during fires, 22
hoses, water pumps, 89–90

I
ignition areas, 17
insurance rates for fire hazard areas, 5
irrigation, 95, 101

L
landscape
    features, 80–85
    managing domestic, 137–138
    managing native, 135

PLANT INDEX

A

acacia, 78
accent trees, 68–69
aeonium, 71
agave, 71, 75
aloe, 71
alumroot, coral bells, 60, 62–63
arborvitae, 79
artichoke, 75
ash, 77

B

bald cypress, 79
barley, 79
bear's breech, 65
beaucarnea, 71
beautyberry, 73
beebalm, wild bergamot, 62–63
beefwood, 78
bellflower, 62–63
bergenia, 65
betony, 62–63
big-leaf maple, 77
bird's foot trefoil, 62–63
black sage, 66, 79
black-eyed Susan, 65
blanket flower, 65
bluebeard, 73
bluebells, 65
bramble, 79
bridal wreath, 73
broom, 79
buckeye, 69
buckthorn, 67
buckwheat, 79
bulbine, 71
bush germander, 75
butterfly bush, 73

C

cacti, 70–71
calandrinia, 71
California bay, 79
camellia, 67
Caradonna meadow sage, 66
carob, 77
Carolina allspice, 67
carpet bugle, 62–63
catalpa, 77

cedar, 78
chamis, 79
chamomile, 62–63
chaste tree, 72, 73
Cherokee bean, 73
Chinese elm, 77
Chinese pistache, 69
cinquefoil, 62–63
clethra, 72, 73
Cleveland sage, 66, 79
clover, strawberry and white, 62–63
coast redwood, 79
coffeeberry, 67
columbine, 65
common gorse, 79
common hackberry, 77
coneflower, 65
Confederate rose, 73
cooking sage, 75
coral bean, 73
coral bells, 60, 62–63
coreopsis, 65
cotyledon, 71
coyote brush, 79
cranesbill, 62–63
crape myrtle, 68, 69
crassula, 71
creeping phlox, 62–63
creeping red fescue, 62–63
creosote bush, 79
crown pink, 75
currant, 67
cypress, 78

D

dadyliron, 71
daffodils, 64
daphne, 73
daylily, 65
dead nettle, 62–63
deer grass, 79
desert honeysuckle, 73
desert sage, 66
desert willow, 69
devilwood, 67
dogwood, 69
Douglas-fir, 79
dudleya, 71
dusty miller, 74, 75
dwarf plumbago, 62–63

mallow, 65
Maltese cross, 75
manzanita, 27, 58
Maximilian sunflower, 65
mayten tree, 77
Mediterranean spurge, 65
mescal bean, 69
mesquite, 77
Mexican bush sage, 64, 66
Mexican evening primrose, 62–63
Mexican hat, 65
michelia, 69
milkweed, 65
mimosa/silk tree, 69
mock orange, 67
moss phlox, 62–63
mountain laurel, 69
mustard, field and black, 79
myrtlewood, 79

N

narcissus, 64
nolina, 71
noncactus succulents, 70–71

O

oak, 77
oats, 79
oleander, 66
oleaster, 67
olive tree, 75
opuntia, 71
orchid tree, 69
Oriental arborvitae, 79
ornamental pear, 69
osmanthus, 67

P

pachyphylum, 71
pachysandra, 62–63
painted fern, 75
palms, 78
pampas grass, 79
parrot's beak, 75
perennials
    festive, 64–66
    gray plants, 75
periwinkle, 62–63
photinia, 67
pig's ear, 75

pine, 79
pine goldenbush, 79
pineapple guava, 75
pineapple sage, 66
plants *See also specific species*
    characteristics of less flammable, 59
    fire-resistant, 33, 60, 70–77
    fire-retardant, 60–69
    flammable, 78–79
    gray, 74–75
    less flammable, 59
    life span of groups (table), 98
    maintenance for zones 2 and 3, 97–104
    safety of, 59
    types of recommended, 60
poppy, 65
portulacaria, 71
prairie coneflower, Mexican hat, 65
primrose, Hooker's evening, 65
privet, 67
purple sage, 66, 79

Q

quackgrass, 79

R

red hot poker, 65
red maple, 76
red yucca, 73
redberry, 67
redbud, 69
rockcress, 62–63
rockrose, 73
rose, 73
rosemary, 79
rupture wort, 62–63
Russian sage, 75
rye, 79

S

sagebrush, 79
sages, 66, 79
salt cedar, 79
salvias, 64
sand strawberry, 62–63
Santa Barbara daisy, 61
saucer plant, 71
Scotch moss, 62–63
sedum, 71
sempervivum, 71

A infiltration basin is an inexpensive and aesthetically pleasing way to divert, depower, and infiltrate rainwater and runoff. See Chapter 20 (page 120) for more techniques and devices for handling runoff to prevent erosion.

Photographed by Tom Zasadzinski

DOUGLAS KENT, MS, MLA

Douglas Kent began work on *Firescaping* in 1992. He lived 25 miles northwest of the Tunnel Fire, which had devoured 25 lives and 2,900 homes in the Berkeley/Oakland Hills area of California. Both frightened and inspired, Kent began to compile a guide that would help prevent others from enduring such a tragedy.

In the years since, Kent has toured, worked with, and spoken to high-risk communities throughout California. He has been on the front lines of wildfires and has interviewed many survivors. With this edition of *Firescaping,* he uses all his years of fire experience to create a comprehensive resource that homeowners and at-risk communities nationwide can use to create more fire-resistant landscapes and structures.

Kent has 27 years of soot-filled experience in firescaping, but that is far from his only credential. He started gardening in 1979 and has written six other books, has worked on hundreds of landscape projects, has helped lead four statewide gardening campaigns, and has taught at California Polytechnic University, Pomona, since 2008. Kent's work can be viewed at anfractus.com.